Albert Stickney

**The Political Problem**

Albert Stickney

**The Political Problem**

ISBN/EAN: 9783337134303

Printed in Europe, USA, Canada, Australia, Japan

Cover: Foto ©Suzi / pixelio.de

More available books at **www.hansebooks.com**

# THE POLITICAL PROBLEM

BY

ALBERT STICKNEY

AUTHOR OF "DEMOCRATIC GOVERNMENT" ETC.

NEW YORK
HARPER & BROTHERS, FRANKLIN SQUARE
1890

Copyright, 1889, by ALBERT STICKNEY.

*All rights reserved.*

"The men are ripe of Saxon kind
To build an equal state."—EMERSON.


"And contemporaneously with all this, the American nation came upon the scene, equipped as no other nation had ever been for the task of combining sovereignty with liberty, indestructible union of the whole with indestructible life in all the parts."—FISKE.

# CONTENTS.

|  | PAGE |
|---|---|
| INTRODUCTORY | 1 |
| CHAP. I. THE THEORY OF OUR POLITICAL SYSTEM | 6 |
| CHAP. II. THE PRACTICAL RESULTS | 14 |
| CHAP. III. THE CHANGES NEEDED | 67 |
| SOME GENERAL CONSIDERATIONS | 177 |

# THE POLITICAL PROBLEM.

## INTRODUCTORY.

CAREFUL observers of the drift of public affairs must have seen of late a deep and increasing discontent, in Europe and in this country, with the practical working of existing forms of democratic government. Even among the friends of democracy it is easy to see indications of doubt as to the success of democratic institutions, considered as the mere machinery for the transaction of public business. While they are still firm in their belief that democratic institutions, of some form, are essential for the security of the liberties of the citizen and the people, yet they are also often ready to concede that democratic institutions may yet not furnish the most successful working political machinery, considered from a standpoint purely administrative.

But we may go even further.

The essential idea of democracy is that the supreme power in the State is in the hands of the people.

That is the theory.

But how is it with us, at the present day, in practice? In this country will any one say that public men and public methods are under the supreme control of the people? Do the people really select their own public servants? Do the people control those servants after the servants are selected?

In short, does this American people, at this day, under its present political system, have anything more, *in practice*, than a right of revolution? It is, no doubt, the fact that when any particular body of professional politicians too far outrages the public sense of decency, the people can revolt, and for a time remove certain individuals from certain public places. But, when that has been done, how often do we succeed in getting any substantial or lasting improvement in public men or public methods?

Our present political system is one of legalized revolution. Once in four years, in our national government, we have a revolution—a great struggle, conducted, it may be, under the strictest compliance with the requirements of the law, for the possession of the highest public places and the public treasury—between the men who are in office and the men who are out of office. In form, this struggle is one between two or more great political " parties," as they are termed. In fact, the struggle is quite as often between different factions of one party. Almost always the contest is one, between persons, for places.

In these great contests all reasonable men agree that incidentally great harm is done to the highest public interests. The highest efforts of our highest public servants, that should be given to the service of the people, are in fact given to the service of persons. The highest public places, which should be filled with men carefully selected with a view only to their fitness for those places, are often virtually bought and sold—for money. The public service lacks efficiency and stability. Public servants lack ability and experience.

It is no doubt possible that these defects are necessary, are unavoidable. It may be that it is not practicable to secure any large degree of political liberty and political activity for the citizen, and at the same time secure vigor and efficiency of administration.

However that may be, there is no doubt that there is at present deep discontent with the actual working of our political institutions. Thinking men are considering whether there is not some remedy, at least partial, for existing political evils. Many of them are beginning to despair as to the practical success of democratic institutions.

But are we not somewhat hasty if we conclude that democratic institutions have yet reached their full development? Is it altogether reasonable to suppose that our ancestors, one hundred years ago, when they made the very first experiment in the world's history in democratic government on any large scale, created and organized a great political system that was perfect, in which there was no possibility of improvement? Considering their work then in hand, they were a mere group of political theorists. The members of the Constitutional Convention of 1787 were merely laying down on paper the lines of a political experiment. No one of them professed to feel any degree of certainty as to what would be the results of that experiment. Each one of them, as far as I am aware, as to those results had the deepest doubt and distrust. Is it possible, then, that their work was perfect—was finished for all time?

Such a supposition would be most absurd. It is certain that time must have shown defects in our political machinery, and that those defects can be discovered, from a careful study of its actual working results.

Is it not, too, at least possible, that the same careful study will not merely discover the defects, but will also give us some light as to possible improvements that are now practicable?

If, too, it is now possible, in the light of our past experience, to discover some possible improvements in our political machinery, can there be any matter more interesting or more important for the public thought?

I propose, therefore, to here submit the ideas of a single individual, on these public questions, for public consideration. They are only the ideas of one person. If they have value they will receive due consideration. They may need great modification—or, indeed, they may be entirely unsound. As to that, time will show.

In this examination of the political problem, in the solution of which the American people is now engaged, I shall consider, first, the theory of our present political system; then, its actual working results; and thereafter, the changes that would seem to be necessary in our political machinery, in the light of our past political experience.

# CHAPTER I.

## THE THEORY OF OUR POLITICAL SYSTEM.

THE main idea on which our political system has thus far been developed has been that of securing the rights and liberties of the individual citizen.

We have not, thus far, attempted to work out, in practical shape, the idea of a large people, organized as a single corporate body, having its different organs and members, its own brain and will, for the administration of its own public affairs. A government, too, has generally been considered rather as a body of rulers who were to be largely feared and distrusted, who might possibly become tyrants, than as an organized body of public servants.

The idea, therefore, has been, on the one hand, to avoid the concentration of power in the hands of single public officials, or single bodies of public officials, and to keep the supreme power in the State, the selection and the control of the highest public officers, as far as possible in the hands of the individual citizens. These individual citizens, too, under the letter and the theory of the law, were merely to be counted, not weighed. One man's voice was to count for as much as that of another. Public questions were to be decided by the vote of a mere majority— by count—of the votes of individuals. The political action thus taken, though often called the action of the people, has really been, and has been considered, the action only of numbers of individual citizens. Popular government has been, in theory, a government of masses and majorities.

No theory of democratic government is practicable under which the public work of any large people is to be actually done, indiscriminately, or by turns, by the individual citizens themselves. The utmost that has been attempted, in the way of giving the individual citizen a direct personal part in the management of public affairs, has been to give him a direct vote in the selection and control of some of the highest public officials, who are actually to do the work. That work cannot be actually done by all the citizens, in their own persons, with their own hands. Nor can they all take turns at it—except in the case of small peoples of small numbers. Wherever the numbers of a people are large, the real work of government must be done by men specially selected. In the affairs of a small town or village it is, no doubt, a possibility to avoid specialization in public work to some extent. The work is small; in a small country town it is *possible* to have every man make and repair the roads in front of his own land; to have the teacher of the district school live by turns in different families; even the teaching of the school can be virtually taken by turns; it can be put in the hands of the daughter of one citizen for one period, and then in the hands of another daughter for another period. In the same way the few other public offices can be held by turns. And it may be, in very small peoples, that all the public work can be done on the rotatory system. No doubt the work will be done badly. Teaching the district school, the nursery of statesmen and of the fathers and mothers of statesmen, is one of the most important works in the State; it demands a rare combination, of temperament, knowledge, and experience, if the work is to be done well—if the sons and daughters of poor men are to have a good common-school education. But public work *can be done*, and endured, in a very small town or village, on the system of turn and turn about. When, however, we come to the public affairs of large peoples, of large cities, large states, and large nations, then thinking men must agree that public servants must be men who are in some way specially selected, for their fitness, to do the actual public work. It can no longer be done by every one, or it will be done by no one. With peoples of large numbers, therefore, the utmost that is possible, in the way of giving power to the individual citizen, is to give him his one voice in the selection and control of those men by whom the public work is actually to be done.

The mere point of *selection* of those public servants seems, at first sight, comparatively simple and easy. It seems, at first thought, a simple and easy matter to select a mayor, or a governor, or even a president, by a mere majority vote of the citizens, even if the numbers of the people be very large.

But, though there seems to be no difficulty in the matter of *selection*, when we come to the point of control, and consider the question of how the individual citizens are to control, not merely one or two officials, but the entire government, the solution is not so easy. In practice, it has been attempted to secure this point of control by the use of the same process—this process of popular election, so-called—using it for a large number of officers, at short and fixed intervals of time, that is, for short and fixed terms of office. The theory is, by having terms of office short and elections frequent, to keep the official under the control of the citizen *all the time*—or as nearly so as is possible. The result is a use of this process of so-called popular election to a large extent and for diverse purposes, not merely for the *selection* of the highest public officials, but also for the purpose of *controlling* them. The intention has been, not that the official shall hold his office for only one short term of years, for that would make it impossible for public servants to gain experience, but that the official is to continue to hold his office, for one term after another, so long as a majority of the citizens shall see fit to re-elect him? In other words, the highest public officials are to hold their offices on the tenure by election. In this way it has been assumed that not merely the selection of the highest officials, but the substantial control of their official action, would be in the hands of the individual citizens.

A necessary result of this attempt to keep

power in the hands of the individual citizen, to have him take a direct part, in his own person, in the selection and control of a large number of the highest public officials, is the general disuse of the public meeting; that is, the disuse of the public meeting as the organ for the political action of the citizens themselves. It is retained in the cases of legislatures and boards and commissions. But, as the organ for the action of the citizens themselves, it necessarily falls into disuse wherever the numbers of the citizens are large, if each citizen is to act in his own person. A public meeting of ten million voters, or of any large number of voters, for the purpose of common deliberation, is not a practicable thing. Experience shows that the largest number of men that can meet in one body, and conduct rational, calm deliberation, as a single body, cannot much exceed five hundred. With numbers much larger than that, common deliberation becomes impossible. It is no doubt possible to have *mass* meetings, of large numbers of men, where great orators can excite great enthusiasm by appeals to the feelings. But for the purpose of common conference and common thought, where men of different ways of thinking can quietly hear one another's views, yield to the influence of rational argument, and come to an agreement as to a common course of action, any meeting of much more than five hundred men is unmanageable. The attempt, therefore, in any people of large numbers, to have all the individual citizens take a direct personal part in political action must necessarily involve the use of the individual paper ballot, and the disuse of the public meeting.

In practice still another result has ensued: The theory has been that freedom of political action meant that the action of the individual citizen should be free from the influence of other men. This theory, in practice, has taken the form of having the action of the citizen secret, of having the citizen declare his will, on public questions of men and measures, by a paper ballot that is secret.

The general idea of our present political system, then, is that the supreme control of all public affairs, of the entire nation, of the states, cities, towns, and villages, is to be in the hands of the mass of individual citizens, who are to use the individual secret ballot, without the public meeting, for the selection of the highest public officials, and that these highest officials are not only to be selected by this process, but that the same process is to fix their official tenure. The theory is, that thus the supreme control of all public affairs will be in the hands of the individual citizens, and that they will also thus secure complete freedom of individual political action.

That is the theory.

Careful thought will, however, suggest that the system, as carried out in practice, involves a very large use of this process of so-called popular election.

It might be surmised that, in practice, this system of tenure by election, used for so many offices, at such short intervals of time, and over such large areas of territory, might cause public servants to give their time and thought to carrying elections instead of doing their official work—in other words, that government might be turned into an election machine.

But we have the theory.

Let us now turn our attention to the practical results.

# CHAPTER II.

## THE PRACTICAL RESULTS.

THE theory has a good sound.

This idea of having the individual citizen utter his individual judgment, once in each year or term of years, on the conduct of affairs by his public servants, who are selected by himself, by his exercise of the franchise vested in him as a citizen of a great republic, and as one of a great brotherhood of men, each one of whom is born free, and who is the peer of each one of his millions of fellow citizens, quite stirs one's blood. This theory of making the highest public servants of a great nation directly responsible to the individual citizen, through this process of frequent popular election, is quite impressive and quite plausible—as a theory—on paper.

Let us see how it works.

The hard, practical experience of one hundred years has now definitely established, as to the actual working of our present political system, certain fundamental political facts. Among them are the following:

1. The system creates a privileged class.

In one sense any form of government must be a government by a class; that is, it must be a government by a body of men who are in some way specially selected for the public service.

But the theory of a democratic government is that at least the men at the head of the government are to be chosen for their worth, on their merits, by the people.

But this is not the practical result that our present system gives. What I mean when I say that our present political system creates a privileged class is, that it brings into existence, naturally and necessarily, though not by any express provision of law, a class of men who are selected, not by the people, but by themselves, who virtually to a large extent control the selection and action of all our public officials.

Bear in mind that under our present political system the highest places in the government, national, state, and local, in other words, the prizes of public life, are to be won by carrying elections.

This work of carrying elections is very large, and recurs at regular and very short intervals. To state it more correctly, the work never ends. Here is a very large number of public offices. The terms of office are very short. Every year there is a large number of vacancies to be filled by this process of election; and it is known precisely what those vacancies are to be. This large amount of election work must be done by some one. The doing of it has the possibility of great rewards. Naturally and certainly it finds men ready to do it, and usually their readiness to do the work is caused by the prospect of the rewards that the work promises. These men who do election work make it their regular profession, their business. In that profession they gain great skill. They organize. In time it comes to be virtually impossible for any man to be elected to a public office except by their permission and with their active support. These organizations of professional electioneering agents virtually control the selection, and therefore largely control the official action, of nearly all our highest public officials in the entire country, national, state, and local. It is no doubt the fact that our public officials, in the large majority of cases, intend to perform their official duties to the best of their ability. As a class, even under the great disadvantages under which they now labor, they do their work as well as they can. But they are not free. Most of them depend on the professional politicians for their next nomination, and therefore for their next election, to their public positions; in other words, they depend on the professional politicians for their official lives and fortunes. It is certain, therefore, that they will be largely controlled by those politicians. The professionals too, no doubt, are, to some degree, influenced by public opinion. But this influence has its limits. No doubt, too, the professionals, in a large majority of cases, so far as is allowed by their personal interests, endeavor to select fairly good men for office. But for every office there are many seekers. Election work must be done, and it must be paid for. So long as the highest officials are dependent for the continuance of their official existence on that work, it is and will be paid for with the people's offices. Whatever may be the general wishes and purposes of the leaders of these great organizations, however much they may wish, as many of them do, to follow public opinion and serve public interests, they are compelled, by the necessities of their official existence, to pay their followers with the people's offices; in other words, to use the people's offices for their own personal ends. These large organizations become virtually standing armies, engaged in a constant struggle for the spoils of public office and the control of the public treasury. Their leaders become a very peculiar specimen of a privileged class. They are not selected by the people. They are not recognized by the letter of the law. They come into existence outside the law, as a certain and necessary fruit of a political system in which a large number of the highest public places are regularly and frequently put up as the prizes to be won in a great contest where large moneyed interests are at stake and where there are large constituencies.

Such a system may serve fairly well for the administration of communities that are small and poor. It will certainly be a failure with peoples that are large and rich. With such peoples it will necessarily and surely result in the creation of a privileged class of professional election workers who to a large extent control the selection of public servants and the administration of public affairs.

2. The system bars the best citizens from the public service.

The best citizens neglect this work of carrying elections.

They neglect it, because they are compelled to do so. They cannot take the time that it requires. The best class of citizens are the men who work, who are driven with work, because their services are in demand, for the reason that they have been found to be honest and industrious. Their time has value. Their private work must be done; and it is their habit to do it well. The time needed to do this present vast mass of election work is greater than they can possibly afford to give. They cannot give it, and they will not.

It is not that our citizens do not take a sufficient interest in public affairs, that they are not patriotic, or that they are unwilling to make sacrifices to serve public interests. This American people has very many and very recent proofs of the readiness of its individual citizens to make personal sacrifices in the cause of the people. But this work of carrying elections is too great, too continuous, and too engrossing. Those men in the community who have their own way to make, their own living to earn, by their own labor, cannot take the time that is necessary to do the mass of election work that now comes on the community.

The result is that, in this work of arranging nominations and carrying elections, the busy men, the working men in the community, find themselves at a hopeless disadvantage. Many of them at times make a sincere and earnest effort to do what they deem their duty to the State, and to use their just influence in the selection of fit public servants. But the men who regularly betake themselves to this work of carrying elections do so to make money. In that work they have a direct personal pecuniary interest. At that work they get great skill. With them, in their own field, the ordinary lay citizen can never cope. It is the old story of the amateur against the professional, and the professional wins. It is the law of nature. It is needless to say that the amateur sooner or later withdraws from a contest so unequal, attended with defeat so uniform, and the professionals have the field to themselves.

I assume, what I believe to be the fact, that the large majority of citizens really wish to select the best men for their public servants. That is for their interest. It saves their money, lessens their taxes, makes life easier and more comfortable—and that they know.

I assume, also, what I believe to be the fact, that the professional politicians who are in office, the large majority of them, honestly try to give us as honest and efficient administration of public affairs as they can—under existing circumstances.

But the professional politicians naturally, as do all men, look out for their own personal interests. They are compelled to do so. They nominate and elect men on whom they can depend to serve those personal interests. The politicians need men who are pliable, and they get them. But the men who will best guard the interests of the public are not pliable. They are made of firm stuff. As a rule they are not men who are what is termed "popular." They are the men who will do what they think is demanded by a full regard to public interests, with little or no regard to interests that are purely personal.

The result is that the politicians, who have the power, who substantially select all our highest public officials, sooner or later throw aside the men who will not serve personal ends. At times the professional election workers are compelled, under the stress of peculiar circumstances, to nominate and elect very valuable men. But in time—however well single public officers may serve the people, however often professional politicians may make concessions to public opinion in occasional nominations of popular men—these politicians will in the end succeed in quietly eliminating from public life men who are independent and serve only the interests of the public. The best men, whether they wish it or not, are gradually retired, or are put in places where they have no real power.

It is, no doubt, the fact that many individuals, who are fairly efficient public servants, in one way and another, under circumstances more or less exceptional, do succeed in keeping their places in the public service—for a time. But in general the tendency is (and the tendency works itself out with great success) to keep and drive the best citizens out of the public service. They find it hard to get in—and, as a rule, impossible to stay in for any long time.

I am here considering ordinary times, times of peace, times when no unusual call is made on the citizen for the sacrifice of his private interests. When war comes, when it is a question of life and death to the nation, then this American people has thus far found many men willing to risk their lives and fortunes in the service of the people. So too, in times of great popular political excitement, in times that may properly be termed revolutionary, many of the best citizens make large sacrifices of time and money, to effect, if possible, the election of competent and honest men to high public office.

But in ordinary times men do not feel called

on to make sacrifices so large. Then most men prefer their own ease and comfort, and wish to look after themselves and their families. In those ordinary times the men whose labor is valuable, who command good wages and steady employment, are not willing to take the risks and discomforts of depending for their livelihood on the contingencies of popular elections, as those elections must necessarily be carried on under our present political system. They cannot afford it, unless they are men of independent fortune, or are willing to steal. They must, can, and will have security for steady employment, at reasonable rates of compensation. A man who is making a fair income, in a reputable calling, may be willing, for a single year, to neglect his private affairs. He may do so even for two years. But to undertake the duties of any ordinary public office for a term of four, or five, or ten years is ordinarily beyond his power. To do so for a still longer term, if he is to perform his official duties with thoroughness, is too much to ask. At the end of so long a time his place in private affairs will be probably filled, and he will be compelled, in a measure, to begin life anew, under great disadvantages, when he is well on in years. Such risks will not be taken by prudent men.

Such men rightly require greater security of regular employment than they can now have under our political system. Rich men and needy adventurers are, as a rule, now the only classes of men who can afford to go into "politics." But men without fortunes, who are compelled to earn their own incomes, cannot afford the effort to enter public life. It is no doubt the fact that many young men, and many estimable men, from very praiseworthy motives, give much time to the practical work of carrying elections. But men of prudence, who have their fortunes still to make, cannot at present afford to touch politics.

There is a further consideration.

The getting of public office, under our present system, by our present processes of nomination and popular election, generally requires either the doing of a large amount of dirty work, or the payment of large amounts of money for the doing of it by other men. All this work, of conventions and nominations, brass bands, parades, and election literature, with the support of the professional politicians, without whose support no man can now obtain any public office, must be paid for, either in money or in kind. Candidates for office must, as a rule, hold themselves more or less at the beck and call of very disagreeable people. They must do a large amount of very disagreeable work. They must talk with the politicians; they must talk with individual voters; they must talk with any one who wishes to talk with them; they must offend no one; they must make themselves "popular."

At times these experiences, which are not agreeable to men of independence, may be avoided by the contribution of considerable amounts of money. Nearly always candidates must make, in one way or another, a considerable money outlay. Some of this money, the candidates perfectly well know, must be used, directly or indirectly, in one form or another, to buy nominations and votes. It is not usually the case that candidates go so far as to pay, or agree to pay, any fixed amount of money for a nomination or a vote. They perfectly well know, however, that nominations and votes will be bought in their behalf, by other men, with money. And if they supply money, as they almost invariably must and do, they are morally certain that their own money, or the money of other men which they repay, is used virtually for the purposes of bribery. They may not themselves technically commit the precise legal offence. They do, in effect, morally become parties to the commission of the offence by others. Turn and twist the matter as we may, this work of carrying elections, under our present system, or under any political system where the highest public officers hold their offices by the tenure of popular election, becomes largely the buying and selling of nominations and votes for places and money.

Let me not be misunderstood. My belief is that the process of popular election, if used in such a form and manner as will secure the formation and utterance of a people's real judgment, and if used within the proper limits, is the best means yet devised for selecting the highest public officials. But that is a very different matter from putting those officers on the tenure by election after they are chosen. Especially is it a different matter from having the political life of the mass of citizens consist of a never-ending series of elections—of all kinds of officers, great and small.

While, therefore, I am a firm believer in the use of the process of popular election, in its right form and within proper limits, for the mere *selection* of the highest public officials, I still say that our experience shows that the tendency, under any system where there are regular and frequent elections, for large numbers of offices, with large constituencies, necessarily and surely is to bar the best citizens from the public service.

3. The system takes power out of the hands of the people.

It is not meant that the people has no power whatever, or that the professional politicians can utterly, and without limit, disregard public opinion. Even under an absolute monarchy at the present day, with the press, and steam, and the telegraph, there are limits, somewhere, which the monarch must observe in his disregard of public opinion. So it is, too, with an oligarchy.

What I mean is that the power of the people in matters of State is very far below what it ought to be, and is so slight and indirect as to make the name of democratic government, as applied to our present government, quite out of place. The theory is that in our government the will of the people is supreme at all times; that at each election the people really makes its own choice of its own servants, in accordance with its own independent judgment; and that, in and by its selection of public men, it exercises a real judgment and control over public measures.

But the fact is that public officials, nearly all

of them, are virtually appointed by the professional election brokers. Except in times of unusual excitement, the process of popular election becomes merged in that of nomination, and the process of nomination is entirely under the control of the professionals. We may say this ought not to be so. That is very immaterial. We have to deal with what is, and with what will be, so long as we keep this system. It may be said that this fact is the result of neglect of their political duties on the part of the citizens. But, so long as we have an amount of election work so vast (and it is constantly increasing), citizens will continue to neglect their political duties.

But it cannot properly be termed neglect. Citizens perform their political duties as well as the system will allow them; as well as they can. The theory on which the system was put into operation was a mistaken theory. Practical experience has proved it. The system makes greater drafts on the time of the citizen than he can afford to meet. Just so long as we insist on keeping the system, and the other conditions remain as they now are, the results will continue to be what they now are. Human beings, the majority of them, will not give their time and labor to efforts that bring nothing but repeated failure.

While the numbers of our citizens remained small, while the number of elective offices was comparatively small, and the contents of the public treasury were small, the inducements were less to make "politics" a trade; the ordinary citizen stood more nearly on an equality with the politicians, and he made a nearer approach to having his legitimate weight in the public councils. But as years went by, as the numbers and wealth of the people increased, our political system came to work out more fully its natural and necessary results; the evolution of the professional politician became more complete, the power of the people gradually decreased, and that power is now so slight that it is not, I submit, a proper use of words to say that we have a really democratic government.

It may be said that these professional politicians are divided into factions, or "parties," and that the people has at least its choice between the candidates and politics of at least two organizations of professional politicians.

That is no doubt the fact.

But is not that a somewhat poor apology for a democratic government? Can a government, for which that is all that can be said, under which that is the real state of affairs, be correctly called "democratic"? Is that the best government — the most democratic government — the one which gives to the people the fullest possible measure of control—that we can devise? Is this the final outcome, the highest result of the efforts of civilized man, in the evolution of free political institutions?

I think not.

Meantime thinking men must agree that under this system the control of its public affairs, which the people actually has, is not continuous or supreme.

4. The system prevents the free political thought and free political action of the individual citizen.

The theory of our institutions is that the individual citizen should form *his own judgment*, on the merits of public men and public measures; that the selection of those men and measures should be a selection made, deliberately, by a majority of those individual judgments; in other words, that the men and measures of the government should really be the outcome of the *thought of the citizens themselves.*

But that is not the practical result.

The practical result is that every citizen who

needs to earn his own livelihood in some ordinary calling is simply compelled to cast a vote for the appointee of one or the other of the two or three large organizations of professional politicians. Otherwise he loses his vote altogether. Attempts at independent political action have no permanent effect. Sooner or later they result in the citizen joining, or rejoining, one or another of the great election armies. He becomes one of the pawns in the game of politics played by the adroit and experienced professionals. Whatever may be the thoughts or wishes of the individual citizen before election, on the day of election, as it is termed, he finds himself reduced to the necessity of making a mere selection between two or more lists of names selected by the different commanders of the different election armies./ He has, no doubt, in his privilege of deserting his own political army and joining another, a slight degree of indirect control over the otherwise irresponsible tyranny of the political generals. But that is very far from having an independent initiative in the selection of public men—and through them of public measures.

But it may be said that though in form the citizen is driven to join one or another of these organizations, yet in effect and in substance this opportunity of selecting his organization, and of leaving it, gives him some degree of freedom, and gives him all the freedom that he can expect.

To this I answer, that, no doubt, it does give him freedom to some degree—but to a very small degree. Whether or not it gives him all the freedom he can expect remains to be seen, and will be considered later. All that I say as yet is, that he does not have the degree of freedom that is commonly implied in the term "government by the people," and that ought to be implied in that term. What he has is the right of desertion. He has, and can have, under our present system of government, no substantial voice in the selection of his generals. In both, or all, these election armies, the citizens, the rank and file, have virtually no power in selecting their leaders. They can desert, and join the leaders of another army. But, in either army, the leaders are selected by the men who make politics their profession. They are in all the armies selected, by the same processes, by men of the same quality, who use the same methods. Whichever army the citizen may join, or abandon, his right of desertion gives him no substantial control of either men or measures, and is far from being the right of free deliberate action that he has been commonly supposed to possess under a government that has any right to be termed "democratic."

Moreover, even this right of desertion is one that the citizen will, in fact, seldom use. Most men do not like to desert; most men do not like deserters. Most men, too, however much they may disapprove the conduct of the professionals of their own army, generally have a great and controlling fear and distrust of the professionals of the opposing army. So that when the day of election comes, the *working result* usually is, that the citizen marches, gravely and sadly, after the same old political bell-wethers, into the same old political sheep-pen. There is this further very significant and almost grotesque feature. Experience shows that many men inherit their political organizations from their fathers, die in them, and transmit the same valuable political inheritance to their sons.' That is human nature. Boys grow up, hearing continually from their fathers and their fathers' political associates praise of one "party" and abuse of the others. The leaders of their fathers' parties they learn to trust; the leaders of other parties they learn to distrust. It is a most singular anomaly, or apparent anomaly, this law of inherited opinion or prejudice, which so largely controls the political action of the citizen, which is, in theory, supposed to be entirely free, and which should be free, in order to make democratic government the practical success that, when rightly organized, it can and will become.

But taking it as it is, as it now actually works, under the form in which we have thus far developed it, in one of its primary stages of growth— will any one say that the American citizen, whose functions at present are reduced substantially to being the tool of political schemers, in the selection of whom he has virtually no voice, has the full measure of political freedom that it is possible for him to secure?

For one, I venture, on this point, to have a single individual doubt.

5. The system prevents freedom of political thought and political action on the part of the people.

It is impossible that there should be anything that deserves the name of freedom of thought and action on the part of a people, under any political system that takes away that freedom from the individual citizen.

But the thought of "a people," the judgment of "a people," under any correct use of terms, is something very different from a mere collection of the judgments of individual citizens, on a single question submitted to them beforehand, to which they can only answer "Yes" or "No."

This, however, is all that it is possible to get, from the so-called action of a large collection of individual citizens, who are not brought together in one meeting, where it is possible to bring forward new names and new measures. Where citizens are so separated, and are thus deprived of the opportunity for common conference, the only thing that is possible for the individual citizen is to say "Yes" or "No" to some specific name or specific measure submitted to him beforehand.

How is it possible to dignify the result so obtained, from such a process, with the name of a "declaration of the judgment of the people"?

The political histories of this country, of England, and in late years of France, furnish many illustrations of the fact that, wherever there are frequent elections and large constituencies, the people loses all substantial freedom of political thought, and is compelled to swell the ranks of the election armies which are under the leadership and control of a new kind of lords. In form, each separate citizen, and the combined people, retains complete freedom of political action. In fact, and in substance, the people has nothing that deserves to be called by that name. It has, at most, the right of revolution—under the forms of law—with a new kind of weapon, the paper ballot.

These so-called elections become only periodical struggles for place, between the leaders of the different professional armies. In these struggles, as they are now conducted, there is a large number of processions, and banners, and brass bands, and so-called political meetings. A great deal of money is spent, and a great many speeches are made. The end of these struggles, which are very properly termed "campaigns," is at best a choice between two or more sets of appointees, each selected by the professionals. Very seldom, if ever, do we now have anything that can be correctly called a selection by the "judgment of the people," if words are to be used with a due regard to their real meaning.

Nor is any other result possible. So long as the mass of election work is so large, and so long as that work controls the disposition of the highest public offices, and of the public money, so long will these so-called popular elections continue to be mere struggles for place between opposing political armies, and the people will be unable to really think, judge, and act on its judgment, as to real public questions of men or measures.

Little thought has been given, in our political past, to the question how a people is to think—as a people—to form and utter a judgment—as a people—having one being and one organization.

But certainly these processes that we term popular elections, as now conducted, judged by any proper standard, cannot be called processes of thought, or deliberation; they cannot be said to result in "judgments."

The situation is most singular. The purpose of our political system is to secure the highest possible degree of *freedom* for the individual, and thereby for the people. But we have tried to accomplish too much. The individual is overburdened. He is given, under our present organization of the State, a work far transcending his possibilities. In form he has perfect freedom; in fact, in substance, he is in chains. The chains would be thrown off at once were they forged by a foreign power, or a power apparently hostile. But they have been forged, and riveted, by the people itself—by its own free act.

It is a most singular phenomenon. Here is a government—in form most free—under which public and private property are really often at the mercy of adventurers as devoid of principle, and of any real consideration for popular rights, as were the worst of the old feudal barons.

Yet we call this "democratic government"; and so it is, to some extent—in a way—inasmuch as we have, under the letter of the present law, the *power* to change it, and it stands by our own free will.

Still the people, as a people, under the system as it now stands, has not freedom of political action.

6. The system prevents the efficient administration of public affairs.

In all human affairs men aim for the prizes.

Election work, then, being the work that captures the prizes, the men who make politics a profession will, in general, give their time and thought to this work of carrying elections. The simple, prosaic, every-day work of their offices will, in general, bring to public officials little money and less fame. They will naturally and certainly give their time and thought to the work that pays.

If, indeed, men had already become perfect, we might assume that they would always do simply their official duty, without regard to the greater rewards to be obtained in what we are now pleased to term "politics." But the men who operate our political machinery are only human. They will seek those greater rewards; they will use the means by which those rewards can be secured; they will do election work.

These questions would be of comparatively little importance if public affairs were small, and public treasuries were poor, as was the case with us when our political system was established, and before its evils became apparent.

But our public affairs are now large. They involve the handling of large bodies of men and large amounts of money and material. They require for their successful administration men of large ability and large experience—especially of large experience in public affairs. When our country was hardly anything more than a frontier, the duties of public officers and legislators were comparatively simple; experience, and the knowledge that comes from experience, were of comparatively little importance. There were less differences in the values of men. Men were, in fact, more nearly equal. In these later years public affairs, as well as private affairs, have become larger and more complex. They demand men of more thorough training and wider experience. With this system of short official terms, aside from all other considerations, it is simply impossible for our highest public officials to get the experience that is absolutely necessary in order to make them efficient public servants.

It is especially in the members of what are termed the legislatures, of our cities, states, and of the nation, and in the different administrative heads, that we need not only men of ability and honesty, but men of large experience. The old saw, that a rolling stone gathers no moss, is as true in matters of state as in private callings. As a rule, men who are to be valuable servants must give their time to work of one kind, and must follow it for their whole lives. That is the law of human nature in stone-work, wood-work, medicine, war, law, and all other human callings, private or public. This need of experience is especially great with the men at the head of our governments. With the mere administrative subordinates, the men at the bottom, who lay pavements and sewers, who carry letters and do merely the more mechanical portions of our public work, the question is comparatively unimportant. Governments, like all other organizations of human beings, depend for their working efficiency on the *men at the head*. The *men at the head* are the ones who need capacity and training; and if those qualifications be wanting in the men at the head of the government, it matters little who or what are the subordinates.

Now under our present system of government it is simply impossible to secure large official experience in the men at the head. Even assuming that in their short official terms they were surrounded by every possible inducement to give their whole time and thought to their official work, it would be impossible for them to get their greatest value as public servants in one, two, four, or ten years. Men grow. Those men who have the most in them grow for the longest time—up to their latest years. The older they grow, the wiser they grow. These questions that are dealt with by the members of our national and state legislatures are large questions. They are varied. They cannot be decided, if they are to be decided wisely, on abstract principles. They require a wide range of knowledge, the study of wide ranges of facts. Let us rid ourselves of this silly, antiquated, provincial idea that any man can be a legislator, and that at that work one man after another can " take his turn." However able a man may be, however much he may have studied books, however long may have been his experience in private affairs, in order for him to be a valuable public servant, in a high legislative or administrative position, it is essential that he should have a new set of facts and a new set of ideas; facts and ideas that he can get in no possible way other than by actual experience in public office; and the longer his experience, the greater is his value to the people.

So far we have made the assumption that the public official had every inducement to use his time and abilities solely in the discharge of his official work, during his short official term.

But have the men in our highest public places that inducement?

Can they have it?

It is utterly impossible. We will waste no time in considering the officials who are merely subordinates. The very large majority of our highest public servants, under our present system, selected as they are by mistaken methods, generally on mistaken tests, do nevertheless sincerely try to render the people the best service in their power. But they are compelled to give the largest portion of their time to personal matters. Their time and thought must be given, and is given, to this never-ending struggle for office for their political friends and themselves. They have not the ordinary stimulus that the ordinary human man requires to make him do his work well. It is matter for wonder that our public work is done as well as it is. It speaks volumes for the honesty and fidelity of human nature. Every man in high public place is the creature of an election. At the end of one, or two, or four, or it may be six years, if he is to hold his office, he must be the creature of another so-called election. But before he can get an election, he must secure a nomination. The men who surround him on every hand are, like himself, the creatures of an election. Like him, they must all carry the next election. In order to get their nominations and carry the next election, they all depend on one or another of those standing armies which constitute the parts of the great election machine, every member of which is struggling for public place or public money. Meantime other elections besides their own are continually taking place. For every official place there are hundreds of hungry applicants. In order to secure their renominations and re-elections, these high public officials are compelled to give their time to the work of securing public offices and public moneys for the members of what are termed their "parties." A successful politician, nowadays, is usually a man who is generous and sympathetic, in giving his time and money to forward the interests of his election army, and of its individual members. Loyalty to one's friends is a quality very admirable. It is largely through the exercise of some of the better human instincts that a man is a good politician. But good "politics" does not conduce to the preservation of public interests. If our highest public servants wish to keep their places, they are compelled to give public offices to their friends. They are compelled to work for their friends. In one point of view that may be praiseworthy. But it does not make them valuable servants for the public. In short, our public officials are all surrounded, through the necessary working of our present political system, with the strongest inducements to sacrifice public interests to private, and to give their best efforts to work which is not the work of the people.

How is it possible for any man, who would otherwise take pride in his work, to take pride in the work of an office which he may lose at the end of any one or two years, and which simple, honest, thorough work in his office will not help him to retain?

It is needless to say that our public servants cannot possibly do their work thoroughly; they cannot give it their best thought and effort. They will necessarily and certainly give their time to election work; they will put their best work where it will do the most good, in the management of caucuses and conventions. In short, we can lay it down as a law of politics—Tenure by election certainly destroys official efficiency, and turns government into an election machine.

7. The system destroys official responsibility.

Responsibility, in order to have any practical value—in order to be of any real practical use in securing efficient administration—must be the responsibility, of single men, to some immediate official superior, who is always in close touch with the subordinate, who is competent to judge of the subordinate's work, and who has the subordinate continually under close supervision and full control.

Let us examine this statement somewhat in detail, and see whether it is not well established by experience—especially by our own experience in public affairs.

In the first place, I say, we must have the responsibility of single men.

\ Wherever work of administration is to be done, if it is to be done with vigor and thoroughness, there must be some *one man* who is responsible for that one work; there must be some *one man* who is to bear the blame if the work is done ill, who is to have the fame if the work is done well. It is now a well-established fact, in public as well as in private affairs, human nature being the same in each, that the division of power is the division of responsibility, and the division of responsibility is its destruction.

In the next place, responsibility, if it is to be enforced, must be responsibility to some competent immediate official superior. There must be, immediately over the official, in close contact with him, some one man, or some one body of men, that is able to form an intelligent judgment on the quality of his work. I do not say that in all cases this superior must be a specialist. But the superior must be some man, or body of men, competent, from training and experience, to form an intelligent and sound judgment on the subordinate's work. There is no way so certain to destroy the self-respect, the vigor, and the freedom of a servant, as to put him under the supervision of a man who is ignorant—I mean ignorant as to the quality of the servant's work.

Then, too, the subordinate must know and feel that the supervision is regular and continuous. He must be conscious that his work is liable to be scrutinized at any moment; that all his official weak points and his official failures may be found out at any time, and will be found out surely and soon.

Then, too, the superior must have full and complete control of the subordinate. The subordinate must know that the superior, immediately over his head, has full control, within proper limits, with proper securities to the subordinate, of the subordinate's official tenure. Supervision without control has value; but it is not equal to the requirements of an efficient service.

So, I say, responsibility, to be adequate, especially in any large organization of men charged with the conduct of large affairs, must be the responsibility of single men to competent superiors, who have the subordinate under regular and constant supervision and control.

Now apply these well-known and well-established facts to the working of our present form of government.

Power, and, therefore, responsibility, are in most instances divided. The administrative heads, in our national, state, and municipal governments, seldom have the appointment or control of their subordinates. We do not have the responsibility of individuals.

But as to our highest administrative and legislative officials, on whom we must, of course, depend for efficient administration, the case is still stronger. In practice it is almost impossible to remove single individuals for their single individual deficiencies. Everything is massed. When it comes to what we term "election day," then the practical question to the citizen is, not "Has this one official, or that one official, done his official duty;" but "Is it, upon the whole, prudent for me to hand over the control of the whole government to the opposite party?" His conclusion is, almost invariably, that he must, at least for this one time, until some more pressing exigency arises, stand by his political colors. The time for desertion seldom comes. At times, when the citizen thinks that it has come—before election—he knows that by the act of desertion he will lose all weight in his party councils. He usually believes, sincerely, that the success of his party, each and every year, is necessary to the interests of the whole people. So the result generally is that he votes the whole party ticket. And so it will be, as long as we insist on operating everything by popular election. The practical question is, each year, not as to the responsibility of individuals, but as to the defeat of the grand old "party." Nearly always, with very few exceptions, the old political charger, when he hears the sound of the old political trumpet, springs into the old line, with his old comrades in battle, and goes through the old evolutions of the political parade-ground. Individual officials are then too unimportant to call for individual notice. Although the citizen may not in the past have altogether approved the acts of officials of his own party, or of his own party leaders, yet there he is, face to face with the alternative of voting with his political friends or with his political enemies. The result is, as a rule, he stands by his friends. And most men approve his so doing. However much we may, in theory, admire and approve independence of political thought and action, yet in practice most men also admire, quite as much if not more, loyalty to political friends. With the large majority of men the last feeling generally controls their political action. In the heat of the great election contests it becomes a question of success or failure between one's friends and enemies; a question of records and histories, of great and glorious political memories, of great and glorious political parties.

The result is that it becomes practically impossible to hold any one individual responsible for his individual acts. Individual responsibility is in effect destroyed. The destruction of the responsibility of single individuals virtually destroys official responsibility altogether.

Men talk of the responsibility of "party." But what does it amount to in practice? Its individual members, and its leaders, are continually changing. If some one prominent man at any time becomes unpopular, and his unpopularity is too great, he is, for a time, or perhaps permanently, sent to the rear. And then when the next election day comes, it is again a question of great parties and great principles. The question of single men again falls into oblivion. No doubt if a party is so indiscreet as to put in nomination, for some very prominent office, some very obnoxious man, citizens may, in sporadic instances, vote against such single men. And the fear of such action does, no doubt, operate to some extent to prevent glaring official misconduct in some individual instances. But, in general, the responsibility of individual officials for individual action is, and necessarily must be, ignored.

8. The system corrupts official action and our entire political life.

\ The only sound principle which should govern official action, as most men will agree, is that every public official should perform each official act, to the best of his ability, with a view only to the law and his official duty.

In practice, that becomes, under our present system, largely impossible.

Especially the appointments to the highest public offices necessarily are made, and necessarily will be made, largely with a view to interests that are really personal. The men who make the appointments are themselves the creatures of these election organizations. Assuming, then, that they have very upright purposes, they generally think that it is really required by public interests that the elections should be carried by the organizations to which they belong. They reason that the men of their own organization are quite as competent public servants as the men of hostile organizations. They know that they cannot keep their own organizations in efficient form for political work, unless they distribute the public offices among their own political friends. At the same time, the number of public offices is very limited, and the number of applicants for those offices is very large. The result is, that the leaders of the successful organization fill existing vacancies with their own political adherents; and they use their power without much limit to make vacancies for the purpose, where vacancies do not already exist.

So far as to appointments to public office.

But how is it as to official action?

At every turn, the action of public officials is largely influenced by the pressure of political friends. Government contracts are given to political friends. The performance of these contracts is judged and enforced by political friends, and not by impartial public servants.

These are not, however, the worst results.

Whenever the minds of public officials become familiar, as they soon do, with the idea that public appointments and public acts are not to be regulated solely with a view to public interests, but that they are to be used in any degree for what are termed party purposes (which is another name for personal purposes), the next step is one often and easily taken. Our public officials, legislative and administrative, are continually called on to act on matters that affect very large amounts of property and money. It is not often the case, as I believe, that the individuals whose interests are affected by such official action directly approach the public official himself with the offer of a direct money payment for any specific official act. They go to the powerful politicians, and employ them. The politicians secure the necessary official action, often without paying, or agreeing to pay, for it in money. The official is virtually their own creature. He is in their power. He holds, by their grace, not only his present office, but his chances of future preferment. Their wishes are to him virtually commands. When money is paid, it is paid, generally, or often, to the politician who holds no office. Often, perhaps generally, there is no express understanding that any money is to be paid to the official. Such an understanding is too dangerous. But the official action is secured, and very often by the use of money. In law, the crime of money bribery is not committed. The official has only obliged a powerful political friend. The effect, so far as the interests of the people are concerned, is the same as if the official himself had been directly bribed with money.

The same result is easily and frequently accomplished in a different way. What are termed the "legitimate political expenses" of the different political organizations and candidates in election campaigns require very large amounts of money.

Private individuals who have business affairs that require, and are expected to require, action on the part of public officials, therefore make it a regular practice to contribute large sums of money for what are termed "political purposes;" that is, for bands of music, political meetings, and the many and large lawful expenses of a political campaign as now conducted. The mere printing of election tickets is a comparatively insignificant item. It is only one item, which comes at the end of the great campaign. The larger expenses of the campaign, the recruiting, organizing, and drilling of the armies, the conventions and processions, the brass bands and the mass meetings, the pay of the state, county, city, town, and ward politicians through the months before the single day of the election, in fact through all the years, those are the things that cost, those are the things that make the main burden of our present political contests, amounting each year to millions of dollars. These amounts have to be paid by some one. By whom? They are paid largely by the large moneyed enterprises whose interests are exposed to the action of public officials. It is a regular practice—regularly understood.

Now, when a man who has made large money

contributions, to secure the nomination, or election, of high public officials, comes before them, or their friends, for official action, what is the probability as to what the action of the officials will be?

Yet men do not call that bribery. There is no direct agreement for any payment of money, for a specific vote or act, or for any vote or act.

But, so far as concerns the interests of the people, what is the difference in the result?

And does the system, which makes such a state of things necessary and certain, tend to promote public purity, or does it put a premium on corruption? The ordinary idea of corruption is one of mere pecuniary corruption. But what difference does it make, in results, whether you buy official action with private money or with a public office? Or what is the difference in principle? There are, no doubt, cases of direct bribery. But its amount is, in my belief, greatly overrated. Even under our present system, the large majority of public officials, I am convinced, in the large majority of cases, intend to do as well as they know how, and as well as circumstances will admit.

But a vast amount of what is, in its effects, money bribery, is accomplished without the parties to the offence being thoroughly aware of the real nature of their acts.

Vast amounts of money, amounts running into the millions, are paid each year for the support of these great election armies. The men who make the payments expect, and get, an equivalent for their money. They are our shrewdest business men. They pay, because it pays.

The results of these great popular elections now depend, necessarily, largely on the use of money. The decision of one of these great contests may at any time narrow itself to the mere obtaining of a few thousand or a few hundred votes, in some single state, or some single city. With such prizes depending on the result, the temptation to use large amounts of money for corrupt purposes is very great. All well-informed men are well aware that large amounts of money are so used. It is not necessary that they be used in paying money for votes to the citizens. Payment to the professional politicians *who lead*, who control votes by the thousands and millions, serves a better purpose, and is not a violation of the law. Virtually public offices by the thousands, and votes of citizens by the millions, are bought and sold for money. What need is there for any one to pay money to individual voters, for a few hundred individual votes, when, by buying a nomination from the leaders of one of the great "parties," it is possible to purchase over five million votes in a single lot. In a recent political "campaign" we have seen great excitement over the purchase of voters in "blocks of five." But what are we to say as to the purchase of voters in "blocks" of five million?

Any single one of these features of our political system, taken by itself, might not work results so serious.

It is the combination that does the mischief, and makes it so great. The law fails to provide any organization whereby the people can act together, as one people, in the selection of its highest public servants. Factions are therefore formed outside of the law; and the citizens are compelled to act with some faction. Then comes this mass of election work, with its secrecy, its necessary use of large amounts of money, even if the uses are only legitimate, and its employment of dirty men and dirty methods. The use of money in elections has with us at all times been productive of evil results. The evils have, however, of late years greatly increased, with the increase in the amount of election work and the increase in the people's wealth. The use of money in carrying elections has now reached very large proportions. It is a rule, now almost universal, that every candidate for a public office, unless in the poor rural districts, has to pay an "assessment" for the purpose of meeting his share of the expenses of these great campaigns. The mere cost of printing tickets is comparatively a trifle. The assessments are always said to be for meeting only expenses that are "legitimate." Every sensible man knows that in one form or another, directly or indirectly, these assessments are used to buy nominations and votes. And as to its effect on the administration of public affairs, and on the public conscience, the one is about as bad as the other. Well-informed men well understand that our so-called popular elections, as they are now conducted, virtually amount in many cases to a mere sale of public offices to the highest bidder.

But it need not go so far as that. Here in the city of New York we have every year the nominations, which are equivalent to elections, arranged by a few professional politicians. And we have to take the public servants that they see fit to give us. It has been often stated, and, as I believe, accurately, that more than once, when the few professional politicians who had the decision of nominations were unable to agree, they have disposed of the different public offices by lot. When nominations are disposed of in that manner, and the citizen has left to him nothing but the selection between two nominations, when it is virtually certain, as it is in nine cases out of ten, that the citizen will simply accept the nomination made by the professionals whose lead he has formerly followed, what is the real value of this system of so-called popular election.

Is this democratic government?

\The practical difficulties lie in the enormous amount of this election work, its continuousness, its costliness, the size of the constituencies, and the magnitude of its prizes./ It is, no doubt, the fact that, even under this system, the individual citizens have some degree of power. They, no doubt, have it in their power to depose one body of professional politicians and put another in their places. When one body of professionals too far tries the public patience, we have times of sudden and short popular excitement, and we depose some single set of professionals. In short, we have a revolution, followed by another period of quiet endurance.

This right of revolution is practically all that the citizens have. But a system which gives to the citizens only the power of revolution, if words are to be used with accuracy, can hardly be termed "democratic." If this process of revolution produced any substantial or lasting gain, the position would be different. But its result, after the primary spasm, is at most only the putting the control of public affairs in the hands of another set of office brokers. "Politics" becomes the art of carrying elections, largely by the use of corrupt means and corrupt methods.

Meantime the professional politicians thrive—a few of them. But even they—the better portion of them, and among them there are very many deserving men—weary of this feverish, fitful fight of faction. They would much prefer, if they could have it, the opportunity of doing some useful work for the people—in the line of their strict official duties. They would prefer, if they could, to give honest work and get honest wages. But what can they do? They are not free. Their life is one never-ending struggle to get office and to keep it. It is not merely a struggle between the professionals of the two great "parties," but between different factions and cliques of the same party. No individual official is for any long time sure of his place. Of one thing he is, and always can be, utterly certain—that is, if he lets alone the work of carrying elections, and merely gives his best time and thought to the work of his office—his official life will soon come to an end.

These results will continue precisely so long as we continue the conditions. Precisely so long as we keep this political system, or its main features, there is no prospect of any substantial or lasting improvement in the administration of public affairs. As a rule, all men do as well as the system will allow. The citizens do as well as they can. Public officials—most of them—do as well as they can—as well as they can, with their lack of knowledge, of experience, and especially with their lack of *time*. Even the professional politicians who are *not* in office—on the whole—do as well as *they* can. One of the most powerful professional politicians of late years in the city of New York is reported to have said that he had during his entire political career " done all in his power to give the city of New York good government." I have no doubt he spoke the truth. In the simple sincerity of his heart he unconsciously used language that might properly have been used by a Cæsar or a Napoleon, and his words were in entire harmony with the facts of the situation. He was in his day and generation a man of large power. He virtually made appointments to public office, and largely controlled the administration of public affairs. The citizens, each year, went decorously through the forms and ceremonies of what they were pleased to term a "popular election." They gravely went to the polls, took their printed lists from their party leaders, which they dutifully deposited in boxes—constructed and locked in strict accordance with the election law. Meantime Mr. John Kelly, who more than any one man controlled the disposal of public affairs and the spending from the public purse, did, I have no doubt, do his best to "give the citizens of New York good government." For he was, as I have always been informed, a very honest man, and a man of very honest public purposes. But what could even he do? Though he was a political leader, he was bound hand and foot to his political followers. He was compelled—against his judgment, often against his wish—to give public offices to men whom he knew to be unfit for their places. It was the only way in which he could pay his election army; and that army had to be paid. He was a believer in what is termed "party government," which means government by organized bodies of professional electioneering agents, who betake themselves to the work of carrying elections because it pays; who are compelled by the force of circumstances to make it pay; who will continue so to do, just so long as the work is so vast, so regular, and has so large prizes.

All our highest public officials are dependent on, and in the power of, the professional politicians. The theory is, that they are dependent on the citizens, and under the control of the citizens. The fact is, that the power supposed to be in the hands of the citizens is really in the hands of the leaders—from time to time—of the election armies; men who are not selected by the people; who are not controlled by the people.

Again we come upon the great fundamental facts: we overburden the citizen; we overuse and misuse the process of popular election; we use a mistaken form of that process.

We have now seen the practice under our present form of government.

It does not in all respects conform to the theory.

The theory is, that this political system puts the supreme power in the State in the hands of the citizen.

The fact is, that it burdens the citizen with a power that he cannot use. It is utterly beyond his possibilities. The attempt to have the citizen take his direct personal part in the actual selection and control of a large number of public officials, in the governments of large peoples, through the large, frequent, and regular use of this present process of popular election, is a failure. At first sight—as a mere theory—it seems quite plausible. In actual practice, when examined in the light of our experience, it is seen to be radically and fundamentally unsound. It cannot be made to work, with large peoples, whose public officials must have the control of large masses of men, money, and material. It creates a privileged class; it bars the best men from the public service; it takes power out of the hands of the people; it destroys the political freedom of the citizen; it destroys the political freedom of the people; it destroys official responsibility; it corrupts our whole political life.

Is there any remedy?

No sensible man thinks, for an instant, that everything can be done immediately.

But can we not soon get some substantial gain? Can we not make things somewhat better than they now are? Has not our political experience of one hundred years, an experience so new and rich, taught us something? Is government the only thing in which we are to make no improvements? Here alone are we to use the old machinery devised by those provincials of 1787?

Remarkable their work was, no doubt. But they were only human beings, with absolutely no experience in the actual working of democratic government on any large scale. Is it the fact that we can learn nothing, and do nothing?

The idea is absurd.

But *what* are we to do? How are we to work out in practice this idea of " government by the people?"

We have not done it yet. Few men in this country, when they give the matter careful thought, will be ready to admit that they are satisfied with the present working results of this first experiment in the world's history, on any large scale, in democratic government. This greatest of all political problems has not yet been fully solved—for all time. We have done a very creditable piece of political work—for a first attempt. We have shown that democratic government, even in its present crude, undeveloped form, is a thing practicable; that it can be made to work. We have made democratic government, on a large scale, a practical success.

But this is only our first attempt. We have merely launched the good ship *Democracy*, christened her, and given her a short trial trip. Much work is still to be done.

## CHAPTER III.

### THE CHANGES NEEDED.

WHAT, then, is the next stage in the evolution of democratic government? What is the next experiment in the political laboratory of the people of the United States?

The question is one of organization. Whenever work of any magnitude, private or public, is to be done by any large number of men, there must be organization, of one kind or another; that is, the work must be divided, and subdivided; the men who are to do it must be divided, and subdivided. Different kinds of work must be given to different kinds of men, having different kinds of ability, different training, different experience. But, especially wherever any large number of men are to work together, are to coöperate, there must be superiors and subordinates; some must command, some must obey; otherwise the result will be anarchy and chaos.

Especially, inasmuch as a State is a human organism, composed of human beings, it must be ruled by its brain, and its brain must be in its head.

Now a democratic State is not an exception to these general statements. In a democratic State, as well as in one that is termed monarchic or oligarchic, some men must lead, some must obey; the people must have a head; the mass of citizens must be ruled, and controlled, if the public work is to be done, and done well. A democratic State is not a collection of men who are all equals in their positions in the State. All citizens should, no doubt, have equal rights under the law. But they cannot all hold the same positions in the State. The points wherein a democratic State differs from one that is termed monarchic or oligarchic, is that in the democratic State the supreme will is, or should be, the will of the people, instead of being the will of one man, or of a few men. But there must be a supreme will, and a strong will, controlled by a wise judgment, if we are to avoid anarchy and a great waste of strength.

Democratic institutions are to win their way, if they do win it, as they will, and are now fast doing, for the reason, not that they attempt the ridiculous impossibility of making all men equal, not because they seek, or will be able, to reduce society to a dead level of mediocrity, but because they will, when more fully developed, give society a more perfect organization, will more perfectly marshal its forces, will more thoroughly subordinate the bad social elements to the good, will more fully enable men to find their right places, will give greater security for having society ruled by its brains—by men of worth, instead of men of birth. The idea that democracy is to be a State where all men are to be masters, or where every man is to be his own master, where all men are to rule, and none to obey, is quite crude and erroneous. In a democratic State, when its evolution is more complete, men will be ruled as they have never yet been ruled; they will obey as they have never yet been compelled to obey. Society will be ruled by a stronger will and a wiser judgment than ever before; for the will of a people is a stronger will, and the judgment of a people is a wiser judgment, than the will or judgment of any one individual, or faction of individuals.

But the chief point in a democratic government, which is, like any other government, or should be, an organization of men, is how to get the brains at the head. Democracy, if it succeed, as it will, will succeed because it furnishes the best security for getting the people's best men at its head. In order to handle these great modern social forces, that are continually growing with the growth of men's knowledge, we must have better government; society must have stronger and wiser control; and that control is to be found only in a more perfect organization, an organization which can be had only from democracy.

The question, then, is one of organization.

The first point to be ascertained is, what are the chief ends, the chief practical results, that must be accomplished, made actual accomplished facts, by any government that deserves the name of "democratic."

Those chief ends are, as it seems to me, three:

1. It must secure the most full, free, and healthy political action on the part of the individual citizen.

Taking it as a practical question, my reason for insisting on the fullest measure of practicable political action for the individual citizen is, that it is the best practicable way to get the best results in the administration of public affairs, as well as the best way to secure the healthy development of the citizen and of the State. It will work well.

But when we say that we must secure the fullest practicable measure of political activity for the citizen, it does not mean that his political functions are to be limited to his being allowed to put "his mark" against a few names selected by him from printed lists made up by the professionals, even if the State pays the printing bills and puts him in a box while he "makes his mark."

The citizen must do something more than that, if democratic government is to be anything other than a farce and a failure.

2. It must secure the supremacy of the judgment and will of the people.

This means something more than having an annual, or biennial, or quadrennial choice, by the individual citizens, between the tickets of different organizations of professional election brokers.

Any government that deserves the name "democratic" must provide some simple and efficient means whereby the people can think—as a people, can form its deliberate judgment—as a people, and can form and utter its will—as a people, on precise practical public questions of both men and measures.

It is not a political process of any great practical value, to have mere periodic countings of noses on a selection between the "tickets" of rival factions of professional politicians, even if there be a prominent protrusion of what are termed political platforms, by so-called grand old political parties, with grand old political platitudes, termed "party principles," so vague that they mean anything or nothing.

There must be some simple practical machinery whereby the people can confer, hold its common deliberations, at the time when it is to act, on the precise question, whether of men or measures, on which it is to act. There must be more than a counting of individual preferences. There must be the means for forming a "judgment" of "the people" by a process of thought — of the people.

3. It must secure efficient administration.

It has commonly been assumed that democratic government necessarily involved some degree of sacrifice on the score of administrative efficiency.

This is, in my belief, a mistake. Taking it as a whole, with all its faults, I incline strongly to the opinion that our present political system, our particular combination of national, state, and local governments, as it has existed during this last one hundred years, has produced better practical results, taking them altogether, than have been produced by any system of political organization thus far known, in the same space of time. Its faults have, no doubt, been great and glaring. We have not reached perfection. Yet even the degree of political freedom that we have thus far enjoyed, and the imperfect organization that we have thus far effected, have, as it seems to me, given us remarkable practical results. When we shall have continued our experiment, in the light of what we can now learn from our past experience, when this hard-headed, practical American people once seriously undertakes to concentrate its thought (as it is now beginning to do) on the present phase of the democratic problem, then our results will be better. Then we shall — in time — demonstrate the fact, by fresh experiments, with new and improved political machinery, that for the purposes of mere administration, there is no form of government so efficient as a free democracy.

Any government, therefore, I say, that deserves the name of "democratic" must secure, with other results, that of efficient administration.

That means, especially, the selection of fit men at the head.

The men of importance in any government are

the men at its head. They are, of all men, the ones who must be able, honest, and of large experience. We have been in the habit of virtually assuming that the administration of public affairs required only ordinary men, men of ordinary ability, of ordinary honesty, and ordinary experience. And it has been often assumed by political writers that democratic government means government by any one and every one, turn and turn about — in short, that it means *government by the masses.*

Democratic government, as I understand the term, means government by the people's brain. It means that the administration of public affairs shall be in accordance with the best judgment that can be formed by the entire people, by its best blood and fibre. It means government by the best men.

My reason for my confidence in democratic institutions is, that, in my judgment, the political experience of the world, and especially of this country, has now established that, upon the whole, in the long run, no other form of government gives so much stability, so much vigor, gives security so strong for the selection of the fittest men for the highest public places as will the democratic, provided, however, the people be so organized as to secure real freedom of thought and action.

This is the point of essential importance, the having strong men, men of large natural capacity, with the thorough training that comes only from large experience, at the government's head. Get the right men at the head, and they will see to the subordinates. As to that we need give ourselves no uneasiness. The point of importance is the getting the right men at the head.

To recapitulate, then, the chief practical results which must be accomplished by any government that deserves the name of " democratic," are three:

1. It must secure the most full, free, and healthy political action on the part of the individual citizen.

2. It must secure the supremacy of the people's will and the people's judgment.

3. It must secure efficient administration.

With a view to the realization, in practice, of these ends, let us next see whether some political facts, as to the practical working of democratic institutions, have not now been established —by experience.

I submit that at least three such facts are now so established.

They are, as it seems to me, these:

**I. The public meeting is the organ for the formation and declaration of the people's judgment and the people's will.**

This statement, in its general terms, might be generally accepted, as a statement of a theoretical principle, as to a people's action on *measures*.

It is equally accurate as a statement of the proper practice, in the formation of anything that deserves the name of a "judgment," as to *men*.

Let us consider the nature of the process, and we shall easily understand its reason and its necessity.

Wherever any number of individuals, having common interests, need to *agree* on a common course of action, the simple, natural, and easy method of reaching that agreement, if they are reasonable beings, is for them to meet and confer. If they are not reasonable beings, then they are not fit for democratic institutions, and are not here to be taken into account. But if they are, if they meet and confer, they will in time almost invariably come to an agreement. Each individual will have his own individual ideas. Those ideas will have to be harmonized. Individuals will have to make concessions. The easiest and quickest way—in short, the only way that is really practicable and effectual—by which they can reach this result of agreement, is for them to meet and confer, to concede and agree. That is the way reasonable men do in their private affairs. That is the way reasonable men must do in public affairs. Each individual will have a reasonable opportunity to utter his own views, to hear the views of other men, and to change his own. In time, the entire body is reasonably certain to agree on a common conclusion.

It is virtually assumed by nearly all writers on democratic institutions that men of different ways of thinking must always continue to differ; that they must hold to their own individual ideas to the end; that men holding like ideas must combine in factions, and must have a great contest once in a certain or uncertain term of years for the possession of the highest public offices and the supreme control of public affairs.

This assumption utterly ignores the limitations of human minds, and human knowledge; the fact that all men are ignorant, one-sided, and liable to error; that most of them, if they are placed under the right influences, wish to correct their errors; that all of them, if they do not wish it, *ought* to correct those errors; and that the furnishing the opportunity for men to learn the ideas of others, and thereby to correct their own errors, is the chief end to be attained under a free democratic government by free political processes.

To accomplish that end there is as yet no known practicable process for any large number of citizens, other than that of the public meeting. Without that process—keeping the individual citizens separate, restricting them to the opportunity of casting a secret ballot separately, without the opportunity for free public conference, at the time they take public action—the citizen is restricted to the right to utter his own separate individual present preference between two or more special men or measures proposed beforehand by single men or single factions. The very essence of democratic free thought is wanting. The most valuable of all the processes possible to a free people is virtually disused. The citizen and the people are both deprived of the chief opportunity that can be provided by democratic institutions, for political instruction and political thought. They become virtually the puppets in a political Punch and Judy, pulled backwards and forwards by professional politicians. The most essential features of a free, healthy political life are lost.

This is so even when we are dealing only with the citizens of a small political body, like the people of a village or a small town.

But when we come to consider the cases of the large peoples—the peoples of the large cities and states and of the nation, where it is necessary for large numbers of men to come to a common conclusion as to a course of common action, as to large public affairs and large public interests— the utter impossibility of having anything like the formation of a common judgment—by a people— as to the real merits of any precise question, of either public measures or public men, by these so-called popular elections, without the representative public meeting, becomes grotesquely apparent. Especially is this so if these elections are frequent and for large numbers of officers. It then becomes utterly impossible for the large majority of citizens to get any considerable amount of knowledge as to the real merits of specific practical public questions. Even the most intelligent, the ablest, the most highly educated, and the most thoughtful individual citizen will nearly always be unable to get the knowledge of the special facts of special cases which is absolutely indispensable to enable him to form anything that deserves the name of a judgment—on its merits—of any special question. He can, no doubt, join in a party procession, follow a party banner, pound on a party drum, and blow a party trumpet; but to form a calm judgment, even of one single individual, on any specific question, by this process of an annual conflict for place between two or more great armies of professional politicians, is an impossibility.

What process, then, is there that will enable a people of large numbers really to think as a people—to weigh the merits as a people—of public men and public measures?

There is only one such process—that is, only one has yet been found, tried, and proved by experience—and that is the process of the public meeting.

This public meeting will be a meeting of all the citizens, meeting in their own persons, if their numbers be not too large to allow them to meet and act conveniently in one body. If, however, their numbers be too large to allow them conveniently to meet and act as one body in their own persons, then they must meet and act in the persons of their representatives. When the number of citizens who are to take common political action is more than about five hundred, they must be divided into smaller primary districts, and the citizens in the primary districts must meet in public, choose their representatives, and the representatives so chosen must thereafter meet in one body, and take action as one body for the entire people.

For instance: Take the case of a people having a population of one million. That would ordinarily mean with us a number of voting citizens of about two hundred thousand. If this people go through the form of choosing a large number of public officials each year through the ordinary process of the so-called popular election, by written or printed ballots, cast by the citizens separately, without using the public meeting, then it can, by possibility, accomplish nothing but the making a selection, by a mere majority of individuals, between the nominees submitted beforehand of two or more strong organizations. We have tried this experiment now for many years, and its results are well known and uniform. The process of election becomes merged in the process of nomination, and the process of nomination falls, sooner or later, into the hands of professionals.

Suppose, on the other hand, that this people of two hundred thousand citizens be divided into five hundred primary bodies in that number of primary districts, giving four hundred citizens to each district, and that the citizens in each district came together in one public meeting and chose a delegate; that then the five hundred delegates so chosen met in one public meeting and chose a chief executive official or a delegate to a state or national legislature. In that case the citizens in each district would have at least the *opportunity* to make their own free choice of a delegate; citizens would have at least the *opportunity* to make new nominations at the time on the spot; they would have something more than the mere opportunity to choose between two or three "tickets" presented beforehand. A delegate so chosen by a majority, or, better, by two thirds, of the citizens so met, could be properly said to be the "choice" of the district; and those delegates, meeting in one assembly, would have at least the *opportunity* to make something that might properly be termed the free choice of that entire people.

It is to be noted that such a procedure would involve merely the adoption, under the law, of the same machinery for the action of the whole people that has largely been already adopted, outside the law, for the action of our present political parties. It is the well-known, well-tried machinery of action by delegates, where it is impossible or impracticable for the principals to act in their own persons.

Is it not plain, therefore, that the only means practicable by which anything can be had that can be properly termed an expression of the "will of the people" is the public meeting of citizens or their delegates?

But I go further.

Not only is the public meeting the proper process by which a people should form its common will, but it is the only process by which it can form anything that can properly be termed a "common judgment," a "judgment of the people."

Again, let us consider the actual working process of an ordinary public meeting, like the simple, old-fashioned town meeting.

If the question be one of passing a town ordinance or voting a town expenditure, if the citizens meet, the action of the meeting is not limited to the simple acceptance or rejection of some measure proposed beforehand. Amendments are offered. Wholly new measures are proposed. Public debate is had. Men utter their individual opinions. Reasonable men change their opinions. Many men then form their opinions for the first time — that is, on the precise question on which action must be had. Extremists are compelled to make concessions, though they may have great weight in forming the final judgment. In the end the common agreement is generally a compromise between the views of extremists. The result reached by this process of compromise and agreement is nearly always something very different from the views of any single individual, or of any single faction, as those views had existed beforehand. This result, no doubt, may not be the wisest possible result. It may, possibly, not be as wise a result as would be obtained by adopting, bodily, the judgment of some single individual or of some single faction. But it will be a new result, the result of a new process—a process that can properly be termed co-operative thought by a corporate, co-operative brain. Such a result will be properly termed a "judgment of the people."

So, too, when popular action is to be taken in the selection of a man, to fill any public office. The ordinary parliamentary practice in any public meeting would be to act on candidates for different public offices one at a time—at least to consider the candidates for each office separately from the candidates for other offices. Debate can be had. It will be possible to have something like the deliberation of a whole people, at the time the voting is done, on the fitness of single men for the work of single offices. Many citizens will be, before the meeting, wholly uninformed as to the different candidates—their occupations, reputations, and characters. Citizens who have this knowledge will be able to give it to others who have it not. In this way it will be possible to get a process that can properly be termed "thought of the people" on the fitness of different candidates. The result of that thought will be something that can properly be termed a "judgment of the people."

Now, can that result be had without this process?

But I go further.

Not only is the public meeting the only machinery whereby we can obtain a "judgment of the people," but in the large majority of cases the judgment of the people thus formed, especially the judgment of any large people, will be wiser than the judgment of any single man or single faction.

Public questions are large, many-sided, and often involve the consideration of wide masses of facts. But the knowledge of each individual, as far as it bears on public questions, is generally comparatively narrow and scanty. Each individual will need information, of a kind that he will, in general, be able to get only from other men.

Public action on public questions can seldom be taken wisely by mere adherence to previously formed ideas, even if they be formed with great care. The wisdom of a public measure generally depends on careful consideration of diverse private and public interests. Decisions of such questions, if they are to be wise, must be made after a calm, careful weighing of varied individual views. The judgments of single individuals are generally made on views that are partial and one-sided, on insufficient knowledge and information. In order to get large, many-sided views of large public questions, it is essential to have the conference of many minds.

It is often urged, as a defence of what is termed "party government," that men differ in temperament—that some are conservative, and others are eager for change. It is then inferred that these two classes of men should be formed into separate and antagonistic organizations, and that these antagonistic organizations should from time to time have a contest for the possession of public offices and the control of public affairs.

I deny that it is possible to divide any community into two factions, the individual members of each of which will agree in their judgments (if they have formed any) on all public questions. But if the citizens could be so divided, even then, I submit, such a division would not well serve public interests.

Public interests demand, not that those two classes of individuals, assuming that they exist, should be separated into two hostile political camps, but that they should be brought together into one common organization, in order that they may be led to co-operate, to confer, and agree—as to the course that is most wise, which is presumably not the extreme view of either class, but a mean view between the two extremes.

But that is not all.

Assuming that it is possible for the individual citizen to form an intelligent judgment on many practical public questions, the citizens, on the same questions, will divide on different lines. In forming these large factions, therefore, which are commonly termed "parties," the only thing that is practicable, even as to single questions, is to select some "issue," as it is termed, which is very general, into which there must generally enter some question of a moral or sentimental aspect, which will serve as a battle-cry and rouse the masses. But the great majority of public questions are simply questions of prosaic, matter-of-fact business — mainly questions of raising and spending the public money and doing very prosaic work. The result is that it is, in the large majority of cases, impossible by these party conflicts to get an expression of even the opinions of individual citizens as to any specific practical questions. Practical questions are questions of fact and detail. They must be carefully considered in detail. Specific measures must be proposed, discussed, and amended. There is no way in which this work can be done, or by which any question can receive the common consideration of any large number of minds, other than by the process, not of conflict, but of conference. There must be, not a struggle between armies for public place, but co-operative thought, of men of different ways of thinking, in calm common conference. Differences must be harmonized, not increased. Whatever conflict there is must be the conflict of ideas, not of persons.

Now consider what generally takes place whenever any reasonable number of reasonable men, who are not under the necessity of serving personal ends, and who are not influenced by sentimental considerations, come together for common conference as to common interests. There is nothing which will so stimulate the thought of the individual as conference with other reasonable men. Each individual is reasonably certain to utter his best individual thought. Its merits will be judged by the wiser judgment of others. The common judgment of the body, formed by common agreement, in selecting from the ideas of individuals, will be reasonably certain, if there be time, to combine the best results of the thought of the individuals. This common judgment will be the fruit of nature's process, the survival of the fittest, by natural selection, by the common judgment, from the struggle of ideas.

Any other process than this one of co-operative conference deprives reasoning men of the natural, simple means of influencing other reasoning men by reasonable arguments. The present system of party conflicts assumes that men who differ in their individual ideas on prominent public questions are to continue to differ; that they are to be kept asunder; that they are not to change their ideas, are not to learn.

Now the essential fundamental idea of democratic government is, that the State is to be a government of ideas and laws, not of persons; that, therefore, the machinery of government is to furnish the most simple and direct means whereby the *soundness of ideas* is to be tested; that the community is not to be governed in accordance with the ideas or the wishes of any one man, or of any one faction; but that the governing ideas must be the wisest ideas of the whole people, thinking and acting with freedom, as one whole people.

Consider what are the ordinary chances of action by delegates of any people of large numbers—provided those delegates are freely chosen, and are free to act on their common judgment. Even the men whom we now send to our national Congress are many of them able men. They are generally men without special knowledge or special experience for their special work. But suppose that they were free to take the time they needed, and to use their own best judgment as to the measures best fitted to serve public interests; suppose that they were free from what are termed "party," really personal, considerations. Is it not reasonably certain that the common judgment of that body, assisted, as they would be, by outside discussion in the public press, would be a reasonably sound judgment?

## THE CHANGES NEEDED.

But most of those men are not the free choice of the people. I venture to think that the people, if it made a free choice of its own, would select a better class of men than is selected by the professionals of either "party." The people of the United States could easily, at this day, with its larger numbers and larger experience, select an abler body of men than the men who formed the Constitutional Convention of 1787. That convention had among its members three or four great individuals. But, as a body, it could easily be equalled to-day by a body of men really chosen by the peoples of the different Congressional districts. I do not mean, or think, that the choice of the people of each district would invariably and inevitably be the ablest or the wisest single man in the district. But let the citizens have their heads, and let them meet in their free public meeting, and, as a rule, in the large majority of cases, they would be very certain to select as their delegates men of strength. No others could stand the tests. The body of delegates so selected would be, as certainly as we can make things certain by mere human means, a very strong body of men. It would be a body representing varied interests, and varied shades of individual opinion. If they could be free, and could take time for common deliberate action—not for party contests—would there not be a reasonable certainty, as human certainties go, of reasonably wise results?

At least, should we not probably get wiser results than we now get from these annual perennial election campaigns?

Are *they* processes of *thought?* I grant fighting with ballots is better than fighting with bullets. It is a process one degree higher in the evolution of political processes than civil war in the old form. Yet it is, in fact, a new form of civil war; no doubt a form sanctioned by the law, as the law now exists; but it is essentially a contest for place between persons, not a search for the truth in the realm of ideas.

I say, then, that the public meeting of a whole people, in the persons of its delegates, chosen freely, thinking freely, acting freely, is the machinery most certain, as a practical machinery, to give us the people's wisest judgment on practical public questions.

I do not assert that the action of peoples taken in their public meeting will invariably be wise. Peoples, like individuals, will make their errors of thought and action.

I do say, however, that in the large majority

## THE CHANGES NEEDED. 93

of instances, the greatest practical security for obtaining a wise judgment on actual public measures is to be found in the use, at all stages of popular action, on both public measures and public men, of the public meeting.

As illustrations of the accuracy of these statements, I need here only point to two pieces of political work from our own political experience: the formation of our national Constitution, and the body of constructive political legislation passed by our national Congress at the very beginning of our political life, under that Constitution, whereby the national government was put into operation. Those two pieces of work I submit to the judgment of reasonable men, as examples of what can be accomplished by the simple process of common deliberation between men having the widest differences of individual opinion. The study of the proceedings of the Constitutional Convention of 1787 is most instructive. The individual members of that convention had the largest divergence of individual views as to what should be the form of federal union which they should recommend. They came together without authority to form a national government. When they met, it is safe to say that hardly one of them had the most remote conception of anything like the scheme of political organization on which they finally agreed, or of anything like a single national government for a single people. If they had met as the members of two rival political parties engaged in a continual struggle for the possession of public place, it is doubtful if they would have come to any agreement as to any constitution. Fortunately they were free. Each individual held his individual views. He uttered them. Many of them he changed. Agreement came, first as to single points, single clauses, and single articles. The combined result, made by putting together those separate parts, did not, in all respects, commend itself to the judgment of even any one individual. But the individual members agreed on that combined result for the reason that public interests demanded that they should agree on something—and they could agree on nothing else. Even after the Constitution was framed, many men who took part in its construction had the gravest doubts as to the possibility of its being made a working success.

Then came the organizing of the government under the Constitution. That, too, was accomplished by the same process of selection and agreement. But this work, too, was done by men who were free; who were not under the pressure of factional passions and factional interests.

Better work can be done now by using the same process.

Why not?

The whole system of popular election, as it is now framed, rests on an unsound principle—the assumption that the individual citizen can take a direct personal part in the direction of the public affairs of large peoples. The idea is, that if the highest public officials, the members of the popular assembly or of the legislature, as it is commonly called, are elected at frequent intervals by the direct vote of the citizens, each individual citizen has the opportunity to pass his individual judgment on the conduct of the official, and re-elect the official, or elect some other man in his stead, according to the nature of that individual judgment.

In the public affairs of the small peoples, the villages and towns, and in the public affairs of the smaller electoral districts, in short, as to all matters that come before what may be called the primary public meetings—the political units in city, state, and national affairs—the individual citizen can take his direct personal part.

When, however, it comes to the affairs of the

larger peoples, the individual citizen must act in the person of his representatives; his direct personal action must be limited to his action in his local district meeting, in what may be termed the people's primaries.

If it were possible for him, under this specious form of direct popular election, by the mere counting of individuals, to pass a judgment of approval, or disapproval, on the policy of the people's representatives, it would not be desirable. For no mere individual citizen is qualified to pass such a judgment. He cannot have the necessary knowledge of the facts; nor can he get the necessary time for thought. On the other hand, the formation of any such judgment is not possible. The attempt to get such a result necessarily results in failure. It puts on the citizen a burden that he cannot possibly carry. It puts on him a duty that would require his entire time and that even then he could not accomplish. The attempt to work out that idea in practice brings into existence this large amount of election work which, as our experience has demonstrated, results in putting the selection and control of our highest public officials in the hands of the election brokers, and destroys the political freedom of both citizen and people.

I do not say that the use of the public meeting, of and by itself, would put an end to the power of the professional politician, and make the citizen and the people free.

To accomplish that result it will be necessary, as I shall try to show later, to give up this entire system of tenure by election, and to so cut down the number of elective offices as to reduce the amount of election work to a point which will insure good administration, and put the control of affairs in the hands of the people.

But what I do say is, that, in order to get anything that can be correctly termed an expression of the people's judgment, or the people's will, on any question, we must use, at every stage, the public meeting.

That is the first fact as to the practical working of democratic institutions, that is, in my belief, now established by our political experience.

## II. Administration must have one head.

That means, that at the head of every administrative office and department there must be some one man, who shall have the selection, the control, and the removal of his own subordinates; and that all the heads of administrative offices or departments in the administrative service of a people, the people of a single town, or city, or state, or nation, shall, in like manner, be directly under the control of, and responsible to, a mayor, governor, or president—in other words, to some one executive head.

This fact is now pretty generally conceded by practical men who have had any considerable experience with affairs and men.

In the earlier rudimentary stages of the development of democratic institutions, it was generally assumed that administrative power, in order to secure the people against its tyrannical abuse, must be divided among several individuals or bodies. It was considered dangerous to concentrate power in the hands of single men.

This assumption was not strange, in view of the experience of mankind with hereditary, irresponsible kings.

It has, however, now been established, by experience, that the best security against the abuse of power is in its concentration. I insist, as strongly as any one can, that the chief executive must be selected by the people; that he must be responsible to the people; and that his responsibility must be thorough and constant.

But if he is so selected, and is so held responsible, then I say that human experience has now made it matter of clear and certain demonstration that full security for vigorous and honest administration can be had only under a single head; that is, the honest and efficient administration of the affairs of any people, small or large, can be secured only under the control of single men, who are directly responsible to the entire people. How this responsibility to the people can be secured will be considered later. But, with that responsibility properly secured, then, I say, vigor, efficiency, and honesty can be effectually secured only under the one-man system.

The reason of this, too, is to be found in the imperfections of human nature. If men were perfect, they would do their work well under any system. But most men, if we are to secure the best work of which they are capable, require the spur of undivided responsibility. They need to feel that they are themselves to have, alone, the credit for good work, and the blame and penalty for bad work. Moreover, it is only proper and just that, if we are to hold a man responsible for actual working results, we should give him the free selection and the full control of his subordinates. He must have their selection, for he alone can know what are the precise qualifications required for the precise work to be done by any particular man of the force under him. Other men might possibly make better selections for themselves. No one but himself can make good selections for him. He must also have the power of removal, for no one can so well judge whether their work is done well.

In short, it is now ascertained, by experience, in public affairs as well as private, that in administration the division of power means the division of responsibility, and the division of responsibility means its destruction. Responsibility, in order to be thorough, must be the responsibility of single men.

We talk of the responsibility for administration of a great political party. We might almost as well talk of the responsibility of a swarm of bees.

That brings us to the question how we are to secure the responsibility of single men to the whole people.

To that question the answer is given in the statement of the next principle.

It is

III. **The popular assembly should have the supreme control of the chief executive and of its own members.**

## THE CHANGES NEEDED. 101

Let us separate this statement into its two parts, and consider them separately.

And first let us consider the question of its control of the chief executive.

The *selection* of the chief executive, it would be generally conceded by all believers in democratic institutions, should be made by the whole people.

If the considerations already advanced be sound, then the action of the people in making that selection should be had in a public meeting of citizens or delegates. Only in that way can the people act on its best judgment.*

---

* My single individual view is, too, that the selection of the chief executive, wherever it is made by an assembly of delegates, should be by a special assembly of delegates specially selected for that special act, and not by the general assembly, which has the general supervision and control. In other words, the election of the chief executive should be by a special electoral college.

This method, it is to be noted, is the method of which the framers of our national Constitution had a dim conception, but which they failed to put in practical shape in their provision for an electoral college. They intended, without doubt, to create a body of representatives who should act as a body, and exercise some discretion of their own in that action. But they did not realize the necessity of having the electors meet in one body, at one time and place. In

If a chief executive so selected had the free selection and control of his subordinates, and were at the same time himself held to a thor-

---

the absence of any such meeting, experience has shown that, in order to insure a choice, it is necessary that there should be national election organizations, with candidates selected and named beforehand, for whom the electors shall vote under a previous understanding—a procedure which prevents all freedom of either individual or corporate action on the part of the electors or the electoral college. Without such national organizations and such previous understanding, it would ordinarily result that no choice would be made by the electors, as it was of course desired and intended there should be.* If, however, it had been provided that all the electors should meet in one body, then there would be the possibility that the electors could confer, could hold common deliberations, and have a free public discussion of the public needs, and of the right man to meet those needs. In a body of electors chosen by the process of free election, all shades of opinion would be fairly certain to be represented. We should have as great security as we can have under any process of getting a man of ability and integrity and of administrative experience. Moreover, a man who should be so chosen by such a body, would feel that he owed his position to no single man or

---

* The choice by the House of Representatives, in both the original Constitutional provision and in the Twelfth Amendment, was intended only to meet contingencies. It was not intended to be the regular method.

ough and constant responsibility—not at annual intervals, but regularly and continuously—would not the security for efficient administration be at least as thorough as it is now? Would it not be

single faction. As far as could be secured by any mere process of election, he would be independent of all factional and personal considerations and obligations.

My belief is, too, that in such an electoral body, for the selection of an officer so important, there should be required more than the vote of a mere majority, at least a two-thirds vote, and possibly even a larger one. There should, as it seems to me, be a vote which should be as near as is practicable to an agreement of the whole people. The dissenting minority should be, as nearly as possible, only a minority of irreconcilables.

I do not say that this form of the process of popular election would invariably give us the fittest man that could be found for the position of chief executive. I do say, however, that, in my individual belief, this process is the one which is, in the long run, more sure than any other to give us an efficient and safe man for that position, one who shall deserve and inspire the confidence of the entire people.

Is it not, at least, as near a certainty as we can often get in human affairs, that a man so selected will be a better man, one more certain to serve public interests, than the men who are selected by our present methods by the professionals, provided he can, after his election, be, as far as possible, free from factional and personal control, and, as far as possible, under the immediate, thorough, and constant control of, and responsible to, the whole people?

as thorough as we can make it by mere human means?

To return from this digression as to the selection of the chief executive, to the present question of his responsibility to, and his control by, the people, the whole people.

That there should be such responsibility all will agree. That it should be thorough and continuous must be conceded.

Now our present political system, even in theory, contemplates only the enforcing this responsibility, to only the individual citizens, at fixed periods—at the end of fixed terms of years.

If responsibility to the people, even only at the ends of terms of years, were actually secured by the tenure by election, there would be something to be said in favor of our continuing this tenure. But, as we have seen, we actually secure, not responsibility to the people, but only responsibility to the professionals, or rather to the men who keep the professionals in their pay.

How, then, are we to secure responsibility to the people?

The answer is, we must have the power of removal of the chief executive in the hands of the people at all times, instead of in the hands of the professionals at fixed terms of years. In other words, we must use, instead of tenure by election, tenure by the will of the people.

Here, as elsewhere, the people must act in and by its popular assembly.

Somewhere in the State there must be a power that is supreme, that has the supreme control of the entire administrative service.

A State, as well as an individual, must have one judgment, and one will, that is supreme. What judgment and what will can be supreme, with such safety, as the judgment and will of the whole people? Provided always that the people be so organized as to be able to co-operate in the act of thinking, to have its own common deliberations, and form its own common judgment. This is the very essence of democracy—the supremacy of the judgment, and the will, of the people. Usually all that democrats have considered essential in democratic institutions has been the supremacy of the wills of the individual citizens. They have lost sight of the fact that it is as essential for a people as for an individual, that it should be one organism, that thinks and reasons as one organism, and that its will should be subordinated to its reason, to its judgment. Usually, too, the will of the people has been hastily assumed to consist in a mere declaration, for or against some single man or measure, by a mere majority of individual voices.

But that is a thing very different from the deliberate thought of a whole people.

Now there is only one way in which the judgment of the people, as a people, can be made supreme, and the will of the people, as a people, be made the absolutely controlling will in the State; and that is by giving to the popular assembly, by a vote sufficiently large to insure careful deliberation (say two thirds or three fourths or possibly even five sixths), not only the power of making the laws and the general regulations for the transaction of the public business, but also the full control, including the power of removal, of the chief executive, at any time, for any cause in its judgment sufficient—not merely for a crime, but for neglect of duty; for a failure in any respect, or for any reason, to give satisfactory administration.

What we require at the hands of the executive is to execute—to do—to carry out the will of the people, to administer its public affairs in strict accordance with the laws and regulations which have been made by the people.

For any one of many reasons the chief executive may fail to give good administration. He may become permanently ill, or he may become merely insubordinate. In any case, wherever he fails, for any reason, to give good administration, it is necessary that there should be some power in the State that can remove him at once. Delay in such cases may be full of danger.

Where can such a power be so well placed as in the hands of the popular assembly? With what body of men can it be trusted with greater safety? What body of men can have as thorough knowledge of all the facts of the situation, or be so sure to make a wise judgment on those facts?

It is to be noted that this power is already vested, as to the President of the United States, in the United States Senate—by a two-thirds vote, for a limited purpose, on a conviction of "high crimes and misdemeanors." But suppose the chief executive is only ill, or incompetent. The responsibility and efficiency of subordinate officials amounts to nothing if the head be not responsible. The efficiency of the entire service depends mainly on the man at the head. If he is to give good results, he must be trusted with great power. But then he must be—at all times —not once in two or four years—under thorough responsibility. There is no way possible, by which this responsibility can be adequately secured, except by having the power of removal, at all times, in the hands of some one man or body of men.

This is the power that every employer has over every servant, wherever human affairs are managed on common-sense methods, in harmony with the laws of human nature.

It is this fact which insures the administrative vigor that we find in absolute monarchies, in those few instances when the man at the head chances to be an able man himself, or under the influence of some other man who is able. Individual officials are then under thorough and constant individual responsibility. But this responsibility is more necessary for the one man at the head than for any and all others.

This means, to put it in another form, the abolition, as to the chief executive, of tenure by election, and the putting in its place tenure by the will of the people.

In other words, we should give to the people, in its popular assembly, the power to remove, at any time, for any cause which is in their judgment sufficient, the one executive head, instead of removing and re-electing him at the end of fixed terms of years. Having a single executive head, the popular assembly should have the complete control at all times of that executive head, for reasons that have due connection with administration. Hold him responsible for administration. Secure that responsibility, as sensible men do in private affairs, by discharging the servant whenever, for any reason, he fails to give satisfaction to the master. In other words, we must have responsibility to the people at all times, instead of to the professional politicians once in one, two, or four years.

With our present form of popular election, by the direct action of the citizen, it is impossible to have anything other than this term system. It is quite out of the question to have the citizens go through this form of balloting every day or every month. It is very costly in time and money. There must be some limit to the frequency of these so-called popular elections. If we have direct voting by individuals, it must be at fixed periods, at fixed terms of years. But meantime the administration of public affairs, while honest, may be very unwise. The dangers of delay may be very great. In such cases due regard to the security of public interests requires that the chief executive should be subject to the power of removal *at all times* for the mere failure to give satisfactory administration. And this power of removal must be intrusted to some body of men in the State. For men are the only agencies that are available.

If the power of selecting the successor were in the ordinary popular assembly, which had the power of removal, it might be thought that there would be for that reason a temptation to the popular assembly to use the power of removal unwisely, or even corruptly.

This temptation, however, would be largely, if not wholly, removed by the plan already suggested, of having the *election* of the chief executive vested in a special popular assembly chosen for that sole purpose. Of course we cannot expect, under any system, to insure the members of the general popular assembly against any and all temptation, from any and every source. All that we can expect to do in that direction is to reduce this temptation to the lowest amount practicable. This we should do by vesting the power of *electing* the chief executive in a special popular assembly, the members of which were chosen by popular election for that one purpose, in other words, in a special electoral college.

The whole question virtually comes down to this: Should this power of removal be limited to the mere cases of crimes?

If it is safe to trust the Senate with the power of removing for crime, is it not safe to trust the entire legislature, or the popular assembly (under the security of a two-thirds vote), with the power of removing for inefficiency?

And can we secure vigorous, efficient administration, without vesting this power somewhere?

Is there any other way in which we can have any reasonable probability of securing experience, with responsibility, on the part of our chief administrative official? We do not secure that result by our present system. Can any other be suggested, by which those two points can both be combined? Can these two advantages be had in any other way than by having the supervision and control of all public affairs, of the entire administration, in the hands of some body of men of knowledge and experience, who can act, intelligently and freely, on their best common judgment, at any time and at all times?

And where can we find such a body of men, except in the popular assembly, in the people's public meeting? The supreme power, the supreme control, must be somewhere. The experiment of putting it in the hands of the individual citizen has been tried, and has given, invariably and certainly, one result, the putting the control of public affairs, the selection and control of the highest public officials, in the hands of the professional politicians, which means, necessarily and certainly, putting it in the hands of the corrupt rich men who pay those professionals, who supply the money.

This proposal, it is to be noted, consists merely in giving to the popular assembly the same power of removing the single executive head that the British House of Commons has of removing several heads of different administrative departments. Now few men have ever said that there was any danger in giving to the House of Commons that power over those different heads of departments. But is it not safer to give to the popular assembly the supreme control over one official than over many, especially if the assembly has no voice in the selection of the successor? The British House of Commons has not only the removal of all those department heads, but virtually the appointment of their successors. There is, therefore, the strongest inducement to members of the House to intrigue for a vote of the House which will compel the resignation of the Ministry. For resignation of the existing Ministry means places for a large number of men now out of office. This power of removing all the department heads would be comparatively free from danger and inconvenience, if the members of the popular assembly were themselves free from the necessity of paying their political supporters; if they were free from the necessity of carrying the next election; if they were themselves independent. And if the members of the highest body in the State, the body holding the supreme power in the State, were to continue to hold their places by the tenure by election, I doubt if we could obtain any very substantial, or very enduring, improvement in our public methods.

We come, then, to the question of giving to the popular assembly the supreme control of its own members.

That means the abolition of tenure by election for the members of the popular assembly, as well as for the chief executive, and the substituting in its place tenure at the will of the people; in other words, each member of the popular assembly, though originally chosen by the citizens of his electoral district, would be responsible, after he was chosen, not to his single district or to its citizens, but only to the whole people, that is, to the popular assembly itself.

This proposition will, no doubt, seem to many minds strange and revolutionary.

Let us see, however, whether such a change is not now shown by our experience to be necessary. In the light of our experience, will anything short of this change serve our needs?

The theory has been, heretofore, that this tenure by election, this term system, has secured responsibility to the citizen.

But we have already seen that that is not the way in which the theory works. The practical result is to insure only responsibility to the professionals, and to such moneyed interests as are willing to use corrupt methods.

What method, then, is open to us? We must do something. We must at least make an effort to find some practical remedy for those great and radical evils. What shall it be?

This question necessitates a consideration of the main idea which lies at the foundation of representative government.

This idea has generally been that the representative, so called, the member of a popular assembly who was chosen by citizens of a single district, was to represent the ideas of the citizens of that district in his action as a member of the general assembly. This idea has been one of the main reasons on which has rested the term system. It has been assumed that the delegate

" represented " these citizens of the single district, and that they should, therefore, have the opportunity to send some other delegate in his place, whenever he should cease to represent their ideas satisfactorily.

Although this theory has been accepted very generally, careful consideration will, I think, show its unsoundness.

Let us begin its examination by seeing what would be the practical working of this change here proposed in our political machinery.

The common impression might be that it would make the popular assembly a body of great permanence, with a permanent membership; that it would be a body of old men—with old, stagnated ideas.

On the contrary, the tendency would be to give us a body of very able, active men, thoroughly in harmony with the most advanced thought of the time, the membership of which would be constantly changing. But this change in membership would be easy and steady. It would be the continued change of single men by resignation and death (not often by removal), and the bringing in of steady streams of new blood, of new men directly chosen by the people. If the people can be trusted (as I believe they can, with proper organization), the men who would be chosen as delegates would generally be first-class men. I do not mean that even the people would invariably make the wisest possible choice, would always select the one wisest or fittest man. But they would be very certain, in the large majority of instances, when they had freedom of action, to select men who were safe; men of good repute, who had had experience in affairs; men of public spirit, who had been tried. These men so selected would be ordinarily men somewhat advanced in years, who had led laborious lives. They would generally be successful men, therefore generally men of some means. Membership in these popular assemblies, if men did their work faithfully, would be very laborious. Members who were honest would get small remuneration in money; and all that they could gain in reputation they would get in a comparatively short time. Many of them, after a reasonable time of service, would ask to retire, and get some measure of honorable satisfaction from their later years in private life.

But assuming that there were, virtually, no resignations, and no removals, death alone would probably make, virtually, a complete change in the membership of the national, or a state, popular assembly once in about fifteen years. At times single individuals would serve for a longer time, it might be twenty or thirty years, or even more. But the large majority of the members would die within twelve or fifteen years. The result would be that the membership would be constantly changing. But the change would be gradual and easy, instead of being revolutionary. Instead of having a large number of experienced men go out and new men come in at fixed periods, old men would go out and new men would come in singly. The machinery would not be deranged. Work would not be interrupted. The membership would have stability and mobility combined. New blood and brain would be continually coming in, and at the same time the body would at all times have a large proportion of members of experience.

Even such a body of men as, I believe, would be selected by our American people when free, still ought to be under constant responsibility to some competent lawful authority.

How would that be secured better than by having the individual members of each popular assembly accountable for their conduct, as members of the assembly, only to the assembly itself?

In the first place, the only men who can have

any full or accurate knowledge, any sufficient means for forming a sound judgment, as to whether or not any member of the popular assembly is a really faithful and valuable servant to the people, are the members of the assembly itself. No other men can see the member day by day—can judge the quality of the man and his work. Those men will be able to form a judgment that will, in all probability, be correct. If they cannot, no men can.

In the next place, if we give to the popular assembly the degree of stability in its membership that it would gain from the abolition of the tenure by election, no body of men would have so strong a merely selfish personal interest to induce them to act on their best judgment as the popular assembly itself. Such a body of men would have a large degree of official pride, one of the strongest practical motives that men have. That is a motive that always exists to a very powerful degree, with men who are members of any permanent organization. Soldiers are proud of their army. Sailors are proud of the navy. The professional politicians are proud of their party. The members of the popular assembly, being human, would have the same kind of pride for the same reasons.

The members of such a body would, moreover, be able to gain a large knowledge of public affairs, and a long experience in their special public work. They would have the opportunity of becoming veterans. Where, but in government, our largest organization of men, that deals with our largest affairs, do we think it possible for men to fit themselves for the highest places in one, two, or four years? When one comes to give the matter careful thought, how is it possible for men to fit themselves for the highest places in our government, for membership in our national and state legislatures, unless by experience? Every private citizen, in every private calling, studies in the school of experience, and knows that he must do so if he is to be a practical and successful man. There is no private occupation of any kind that a man can learn in two years, unless it be to dig dirt or break stone. Even digging dirt and breaking stone, if they are to be done well, require training of more than two years, for a man must have his muscles developed by years of hard work. But to be a good blacksmith, or a good carpenter, takes long training, long experience; and each fresh year adds to the skill and worth of the workman. Yet our present political system is founded, virtually, on the assumption that, in matters of government, training and experience have no importance for the men at the head. Most men agree that the subordinates—the men who handle letters in a post-office, or who weigh merchandise in a custom-house, or who use ships and rifles and artillery—must have training and experience.

But how is it as to the men at the head?

Where is it that we must especially have the brains, and the power that comes from training alone?

The trouble is deep-seated. It comes from the assumption—that lies at the foundation of our whole political system—that "government by the people" means government by the individual citizens; that those individual citizens are to "take turns" at the public work; and that the individual citizens are themselves, in their own persons, to exercise the supreme control over the actual administration, not only of the local affairs of the small peoples, but also of the larger affairs of cities, states, and the nation. My position is this: I draw no distinction, as to this point, between citizens who are termed educated and well-informed, and those who are termed uneducated and ill-informed. As to this point, of taking a direct personal part in the administration of the public affairs of the larger peoples, *all* citizens are uneducated and ill-informed. The ordinary citizen must necessarily be unable to get the knowledge that is absolutely necessary to enable him to judge of the quality of the public work of any of our highest public servants. In the original selection of those highest servants, each citizen should, as I have stated, have his one free voice. But as to passing judgment, through this process of so-called popular election, on the quality of the servants' work, after they take their seats in the popular assembly, the ordinary citizen, whoever he may be, high or low, rich or poor, learned or unlearned, must necessarily be unable to form an intelligent judgment.

The idea, therefore, that the delegate in the popular assembly is the "representative" of the *ideas* of the individual citizens of the district which elects him rests, I submit, on unsound political views. The popular assembly should be an assembly *of the whole people*, met to confer on the affairs of the *whole people*, and to decide public questions with a view to the interests of the *whole people*. It should be an assembly where the thought of each individual citizen, as far as may be, is to be represented *in the process of forming* the thought of the people as to the practical measures demanded by the common weal. But individual interests and local interests, whenever necessary, are to be sacrificed for the common good. The time when they should be so sacrificed, and the extent to which they should be sacrificed, can be determined, wisely and rightly, only in the common assembly, by its common judgment. That common judgment, when formed, until it is modified or reversed by the same authority, must be conclusive. For his individual action, in assisting to form that common judgment, it is not expedient, nor is it, in the long run, for the interest of any one, that the individual member should be held responsible to any authority other than that of the body itself. When the representative is once chosen, he should be the servant of the whole people, to care for the interests of the whole people, responsible only to the whole people. No individual, or body of individuals, or single section, or single faction of the people, should thenceforth have over him any supervision or any control.

Especially is it against the interests of the individual citizens that the delegate should simply "represent" the ideas of the citizens of his own district, or a majority of them. The purpose of free democratic institutions is to have the general policy of the government as wise as it is possible to make it by the combined wisdom of the entire people. This is the wish of all sensible men. The interests of the whole people, if they are rightly understood, are harmonious. If a proper understanding is had of the interests of different individuals and sections, there is no conflict between them for any long time. But, however that may be, the delegate is chosen because he is one of the able men of his district, much abler than the majority. But he is not infallible, nor are his constituents. Neither their ideas nor his can be assumed to be absolutely right, even with a view only to forwarding the mere sectional interests of his one district. Now, can it be well to bind the delegate, on any subject, so that he shall not have the right to freely change his mind? Can it be wise even to make the attempt? Is it for the real interest of the State, or of any considerable number of citizens, that the delegate should be so bound? To hold that the delegate should be fettered by pledges is, so far, to prevent the working of free thought. The popular assembly is not free in its action unless each one of its members is free to think his own thought, to utter it in his own way, and to change his opinions when convinced by reasonable argument. It is of the very essence of free democratic institutions that the thought and action of the delegate should be as free as that of the citizen.

But fortunately there are few practical questions on which the attempt to bind the delegate by pledges is ever made. As a matter of practice, he is usually trusted to act on his own judgment, as he should be.

The more we consider this idea, that the member of the popular assembly is the representative of any one district, or of any section of individuals, the more clearly we shall see that it is radically unsound in theory and impossible of practice.

If it were possible, *in practice*, to secure this responsibility to the individual citizens, or to any single section, then this idea of such a responsibility would stand on stronger grounds.

But it cannot be carried out in practice. The attempt has been made, in this country and in other countries, in times modern and times ancient. It has always failed. It has secured responsibility to election managers, not to the people. It has secured responsibility only in word, not in deed. It has given lip service, and not faithful work. It has brought into existence a class of noisy men, who prate about platforms and principles, but who are compelled to serve the personal interests of themselves and their fellow-professionals. It has given to the people demagogues and not statesmen—the rule of money, instead of the rule of ideas.

But the most important point is yet to be named.

This change in the tenure is the only way in which we can secure, in the popular assembly, freedom—with responsibility. We believe in free democratic institutions, because we believe in the power and the wisdom of free thought. Freedom of thought and freedom of political action cannot be had, either on the part of the citizen or the public servant, so long as we keep this tenure by election. It is tenure by election that brings into existence these great standing armies, which, under the form of extremely democratic institutions, in effect destroy the political freedom of the citizen, and make our highest public officials not the servants of the people, but the slaves of the election machine. If we are to expect wise legislation and efficient supervision of public affairs at the hands of the popular assembly, its members must be free—to form and utter each man his own individual opinions, to take part in free public conference, to be influenced by free public argument, and to agree, without fear or favor of any individual, or body of individuals, outside the assembly, in a common conclusion.

Publicity, in its modern sense, political daylight, is the surest protection for the people. Bribery statutes do no harm; they never have done much good. But the real protection against bribery and corruption must be found in freedom—and publicity, with real, substantial responsibility *to the people.* These combined will purify the political waters, and will produce a more highly educated standard for official action—in time. It will take time, but not a very long time, as times should be measured in the lives of nations.

But we must bear it well in mind that honesty never yet was the child of slavery—even in governments.

I do not mean that the abolition of tenure by election will abolish selfishness, or bring in immediately the millennium. The fact is, that the real difficulty with this present system of tenure by election is that it is suited only to the millennium; that, so long as men are such as they are, selfish and imperfect, it cannot be made to work well under our present changed conditions; it seems plausible, as a matter of theory, but it can no longer stand the tests of actual practice. So long as we make it for the personal interests of our public servants to carry elections, they will carry elections. And so long as men continue to be influenced largely by their own views of their own interests, it will be necessary for us to make this fundamental change in our government, in order to make their personal interests coincide with the interests of the public, and thereby secure their devotion to the interests of the public. In other words, under our present system, we make an " irrepressible conflict " between the representative's personal interest and his public duty. We must make those two things harmonize.

The actual working of the machinery, as found by experience, is this : When representatives are compelled to carry the next election in order to preserve their political life, the pressure of personal interests will, very surely, in the large majority of cases, make the representative serve the interests of the men who control the organizations of professional election brokers; that means the men who provide the party funds. Those men who hold the money-bags have him largely under their control. To the citizen he gives his profession of faith in the political platforms. To the men who provide the money—

the sinews of war—for these election campaigns, he gives his actual service. If, on the contrary, he is responsible only to the popular assembly, he is dependent on a body of men who are, as nearly as men can be, independent; who have the ability and the opportunity to judge him accurately and fearlessly. If any body of men in the entire community can be depended on to judge him justly, it is that body of men. No other body would be so able or worthy of trust. If the citizens can be trusted to select their representatives, those representatives can, and must, be trusted to judge their fellow-members.

This proposal would give the popular assemblies no power that they do not already have. It is the ordinary law that legislative houses have the right to expel any member by a two-thirds vote. All that is here proposed is to destroy "tenure by election," so as to insure to the members of these supreme bodies experience, and independence of the corrupt elements in the State.

We must realize, in politics, the strong points, and the weak ones, of human nature. Most men try to do right, to live up to their lights. Most men, too, are influenced by their own views of their own interests. What we wish from these men whom we place *at the head* of our public service, is the best service *they* can give us. If we expect to get that service at their hands, we must *make it pay* for them to give us their best service, instead of making it pay for them to sacrifice the interests of the people to the interests of the office brokers. In other words, we must pay them liberally in money (cheap labor is poor labor, in public as well as in private affairs); and we must make the prizes of public life depend on fearless public work, instead of the dirty work of pulling the wires of the political puppets, managing caucuses, and paying for election work with public office and with money. When we begin to carry on our government on those simple common-sense business principles, then we shall *make a beginning* in the work of putting straight the present crooked condition of public affairs. What is now termed "Civil Service Reform" consists mainly of an attempt to take "out of politics" a limited number of subordinate places. But the offices that must be taken "out of politics" are the offices at the head. For "politics" now means the trade of office brokerage. Nothing substantial can ever be accomplished, nor can we even make a substantial beginning of any substantial improvement, so long as we retain this system of slavery for the men at the head. There is the chief evil; there we must apply the remedy.

Notwithstanding these considerations, however, there will still remain, in the minds of many men, a fear of what will be called an assembly of members who hold office "for life." The fear will be that such a body of men will form corrupt combinations, and will sacrifice the interests of the people to their own personal interests; perhaps even to the extent of attempting to undermine or destroy the liberties of the citizen and of the people.

This point certainly deserves the most careful consideration.

First, however, it is to be noted that this sacrifice of the interests of the people to the interests of the office-holder is the chief evil under our present system; and is the principal pressing reason why the system must be changed. The question here is, therefore, not whether the danger will exist at all, if our system be changed, but whether it will be greater or less than it is now.

This question is one that goes to the very essence of democratic institutions.

It is a fact, as we well know, that in every community, under every form of government, citizens can be found who can be trusted to serve the people faithfully, and, if necessary to that end, to sacrifice their own personal interests, their lives, and their fortunes. This American people, especially, has always had such men in abundant numbers. The question, then, really comes down to this: Can we trust, not our public servants, but the people? Can we depend on the people, to find out these men, and put them in the people's highest places? If we can, then the question is answered.

Now the essential fundamental fact on which democratic institutions must stand, if they are to stand at all, the fact on which alone democratic government can and must justify its existence, is that *the people can be trusted* to do this very thing. If the people cannot be trusted, it has no right to rule; if it cannot be trusted to select the men who are to fill the highest places in the State, it can be trusted to do nothing. I agree that no body of election brokers, able as many of them are, honest as many of them are, public-spirited as many of them are, can be trusted to exercise the supreme power in the State, even though they be restrained by the fear of the newspapers. I agree, too, and insist, that, if the people is to select its own servants, it must be so organized that it can think and form its own judgment, at the time it makes that choice. I agree, too, and insist, that the idea that the people can perform the work of administration in any way other than by the hands of men specially selected for that work is an impracticable idea. But in the honesty, and common-sense, and political wisdom of the people, when it is so organized that it can think with its own brain, I have, for one, the highest confidence. It must be content with only exercising the supreme supervision and control. It must act through its members and organs. It must not try to have each one of its members, much less each one of its individual cells, the citizens, exercise every function in the State. Each citizen cannot at once be the brain, liver, and stomach of the body politic. But the people, properly organized, can be fully trusted, when they cease to turn politics into a mere gambling game of political see-saw, to do the rational work of rational government.

But, then, when I say that we can trust the people to select its servants, I say also that the people must trust those servants after the servants have been selected.

We are compelled to trust men—under any system of government. We do it now. We must do it always. What is it even now, under our present system of government, where the people have no substantial control of public men and measures, that constitutes our only substantial security for the honest administration of public affairs? The *consciences* of men; of the professional politicians; their sense of right and wrong. These professional politicians are very shrewd; they understand the political position better than any other class of men in the community; they know very well that it is easy for members in the state and national legislatures to do the work of the large moneyed interests quietly, secretly, and efficiently, year after year, and be reelected term after term, so long as they make fine speeches about the rights of the slave, the rights of the laboring man, the wrongs of capital, the necessity of temperance—in short, so long as they will stand on high moral "platforms" and take high moral ground on all the "burning issues." These men know very well that "politics," as now practised, is a game and a sham. Yet the large majority of these very professionals do as good work for the people as is allowed by their knowledge, their surroundings, and especially by the amount of time at their disposal. Why? Simply for the reason that, after all is said and done, the members of our state and national legislatures, selected as they are, not by the people, but by the professional politicians, controlled as they are, not by the people, but by the professional politicians, yet have *consciences;* they are men of ordinary honesty and ordinary intelligence; they represent a large number of diverse interests; in a rough way, they deliberate, and form a common judgment; in a rough way, under very difficult circumstances, they do the people's thinking, as well as they can; and, as far as circumstances permit, they act up to their best lights, their highest standards. The standards, often, are not very high. The men are taught in a bad school, the one where we now compel them to study, the school of the election machine. The methods are not the best methods. But they are the methods we compel them to use. The fact that our results are no worse, that our public affairs are administered as well as they are, is the strongest evidence of the nobility of human nature, and of the high degree of confidence that we might safely place in other men, selected by other processes, or even in these same men, if, even now, we were to send them to a new school. For the men are very American, very clever, very quick to learn.

## THE CHANGES NEEDED. 135

The matter comes down finally to this: Under the system of "tenure by election" we trust power to these men selected by the election machine for a short term. Under a system of "tenure by will of the people" we should trust men selected by the people for no term, only for so long as the people itself should think it wise.

Under which system are the probabilities of honest and efficient administration the greater?

But it may still be said that this will make public officers hold office for life, and will, therefore, not be democratic.

Let us see what there is in this point.

If the people really makes its own choice of its own highest officials, and has the power of removing them whenever it sees fit, it will have as thorough practical control of public officials and public affairs as is possible; certainly much greater than it has now.

But it is the fact that, with the modifications here proposed, while the control of public men and public measures would be at all times in the hands of the people, many men who entered the public service would stay in it for life. Not, indeed, in the same places. Men who went in at the bottom would have some fair possibility of rising to the top, of winning high rank by good work—as they do now in private affairs. But, no doubt, many public servants would, under a common-sense organization of the public service, stay in it for life.

But that is a uniform condition of the highest success. Men who achieve any substantial success in any calling must follow that calling, as a rule, for life. That is a necessity that arises from the finite nature of man's faculties. Men who work on the rotatory system generally do work of little or no value. The rotatory system is admirably fitted for stars, but not for human beings. In times past, yielding to the needs of our crude frontier life, we have been in the habit of admiring men who were "handy," as the term is; men who could do a little of everything, who could do everything equally well—and equally ill. But we now live under other conditions, and must use other methods. Work must be subdivided; men must be organized; and they must give their time mainly to work of one kind. There is in this nothing new. Men have always done so in large and civilized peoples. We, in our turn, are now becoming a large and civilized people; and we must live accordingly. In affairs of State, as in private affairs, we must generally employ servants who work for life.

It may be said, too, that these changes will create an office-holding class; that we shall have an aristocracy.

That is, no doubt, true—we should, no doubt, then have an office-holding class.

But we have it now. And the question is, whether we will have an aristocracy or a kakistocracy—whether we will be governed by the best or the worst elements in the community. As things now are, it may at any time happen that the office of President of the United States, or Governor of the State of New York, or Mayor of the City of New York, may be bought by the purchase of a few thousand votes. More than that number can be, and is, bought and sold, for money, at every annual election. Under this wonderfully organized, highly developed system of carrying elections, with large numbers of voters voting at the same time for the same officers, through large districts, these skilful professionals know precisely where are the weak and doubtful spots on which they must concentrate their work, and, above all, their money. In the large cities there will be, yet for some time, a considerable number of men who belong to the criminal classes. These members of the criminal classes are the men who buy and sell votes. Under our present system, therefore, the largest possible weight is given to the criminal classes. Other men vote on their convictions. These men buy and sell nominations and votes for money. And thus it happens that these men, who can easily be induced by money to go on either side, or rather on the side that will pay most, are very often, and much more often than any other class of men in the community, the force that in the end proves to be the controlling force. It is not necessary to go into particulars. The professionals, in both of what we term the great "parties," are men of the same kind, and are compelled, in self-preservation, to use the same methods. They have to fight fire with fire. The result is that, under our present system, we give a very undue weight to our criminal classes, and they have become a very powerful element in the selection and in the control of our public officials. So, I say, the question is whether we will have an aristocracy or a kakistocracy.

Let us not be afraid of a name.

Any real democracy will be an aristocracy— the only possible aristocracy. No hereditary system can give a real aristocracy—where men are selected for the highest places in the State for worth and not birth. The only political system under which this is possible is a democracy, if the men at the head of the State are selected by the judgment and brain of the people. I do not say that such men will always be so selected, even where the people controls. I do say that such men cannot be selected, as a rule, under any other system, and that they will be selected, as a rule, under a real democracy. Under the hereditary system the accidents of birth will occasionally produce men of exceptional power, and of large and generous public views. As a rule, however, the descendants of kings soon become weak or tyrannical, or both. The system is a failure. The rotatory system—the system of the political whirligig—is now also shown to be a failure. Whether or not the democratic system can succeed remains to be seen.

For one, I think it will.

But what else can we try? Or shall we continue to use the political see-saw?

My conclusion, then, as to this point of our inquiry, is, that three fundamental principles have now been established, especially by our experience in the last hundred years, to be essential to the harmonious and successful working of democratic institutions; and that those principles are:

I. The popular assembly, or public meeting, is the organ whereby any people, that is, any number of individuals who are to take combined political action, must form and utter its common judgment and its common will.

II. Administration, the execution of a people's policy, must have one head.

III. The popular assembly of each people must have the supreme supervision and control of all its public affairs, of its administrative methods, of the administrative head, and of its own members.

Let us now take one step further in our study, and see what would be the effect, on the political life of the individual citizen, and of the people, of the adoption in practice of these principles, when taken in combination.

In the first place there would be *at least a tendency* to secure freedom of political thought and political action on the part of the citizen.

I admit that, even as things now are, the citizen has, *to some extent*, freedom of thought. He has, no doubt, in law the right, and in fact the power, to *think* as he will on any and all political questions at all times. But though he has in law that right, and in fact that power, the practical working of things now is, that the right and power are unused at the very time when the citizen comes to exercise his functions as a citizen, that is, at the time of election. At other times he thinks with some degree of freedom. At that time he enters into voluntary servitude. Bear in mind that, except in the affairs of the smallest local organizations, the outside practicable limit of action that can be open to the individual citizen is, that he may take part in the mere *selection* of the highest officials. It is impossible for him to do more than that, under any system whatever that can be made to work. Now, under our present machinery, whatever the citizen may think before election, when election comes he is practically certain, in the large majority of cases, to surrender his own individual judgment, and to act with his old comrades in battle under his old generals. In other words, he acts at that time not on his judgment, but in accordance with his feelings, of distrust of his old political enemies, and loyalty to his old political friends. In practice, he then omits to exercise the right that he has under the law, the exercise of which, at all times, and under all circumstances, lies at the foundation of democratic institutions. It makes comparatively little difference how a citizen thinks, or how much freedom of thought he has, under the law, before the time of action, if he is always to omit using it when the time of action has come.

But let us see how it would be if we were to adopt in our government the principles just stated. One effect, at least, would be this: it would tend to destroy the work and the power of the election machine. The work would cease to pay. The number of offices to be filled by the process of election would be reduced to the smallest possible number, and no one could tell when even those few offices would be vacant. For each people, the people of a town, city, state, or the nation, there would be only one elective administrative officer, the single administrative head. Each election district would also have to choose a delegate, whenever that became necessary for the purpose of selecting members of any one of the different popular assemblies. This decrease in the frequency of elections for each single office, combined with the decrease in the number of elective offices, would *at least have a tendency* to bring the measure of this election work somewhere near to the possibilities of the ordinary citizen. The paucity and uncertainty of the prizes to be won by election work would tend, too, to drive the professionals into other occupations.

What now keeps these election armies in existence is the fact that there are these thousands of vacant offices each year, to be gained by success in these great election contests. Once in two or three years there is the possibility of making a clean sweep of nearly all local offices; once in one, two, or three years there is the same possibility as to the offices of every state; and once in four years there is the same possibility as to the offices of the nation. Just so long as these great campaigns are to be fought at fixed periods, and these great prizes are to be won by winning the campaigns, so long the armies will be maintained and paid. Just so long, too, as the constituencies are so large, and the election machinery is so vast, these campaigns will be very costly, in time and money, and will become, and remain, contests in which only these large permanent organizations of highly drilled and disciplined professionals will have any possibility of success. When, however, elective offices are so few, and especially when no one can foresee when any particular office is to be vacant, then the office brokers will betake themselves to some employment of which the rewards are more numerous and certain.

Ordinary citizens will then have something

more nearly approaching a *possibility* of taking part in the act of an election on terms more nearly equal, and accomplishing some substantial result with the expenditure of a reasonable amount of time. Then, as now, individuals will differ in the degree of interest they take in, and the time they will give to, "politics." But there will be something approaching a *possibility* for ordinary men to have a reasonable degree of weight, for legitimate reasons, in the selection of our public servants.

I do not mean that there will then be no "parties," if that term be used to mean merely combinations of citizens for the purpose of concerted political action. Whenever there shall be any public question of sufficiently wide public interest, men will combine, in legitimate ways, to use legitimate means to have their views carried into effect in the administration of public affairs. If at such times it should happen that members of some popular assembly were to be elected, no doubt the views of candidates on such public questions would have due weight in determining the popular vote.

What I am opposing is the existence of these standing armies of office brokers and place hunters, and the political system of which they are the necessary and certain perennial fruits.

Nor need there be any fear lest the adoption of the changes here suggested would unduly lessen the political functions of the citizen.

On the contrary, the sphere of activity of the citizen and his political influence would be greatly enlarged. Instead of merely putting a printed list into a box, with or without "his mark," being himself boxed or unboxed, he would have at least *the opportunity* to take part in public meetings, established by law, of all the citizens, where the real questions on which he was to act would be publicly discussed, at the time when he was to act upon them. He would have at least his equal *opportunity* to take part in these discussions. If he did not take an active part in them, he could at least hear them. He would have at least an *opportunity* to gain, at the time when he was to act, information, not merely from men of his own "party," but from men of all parties, as to the fitness of all the candidates for all the offices for whom he was to utter his voice. If, according to ordinary parliamentary procedure, only candidates for one office should be considered at one time, then there would be at least the *possibility* that each citizen would freely form his own judgment, and act on it. If, too, according to ordinary parliamentary procedure, each citizen were compelled on the demand of a reasonable number of citizens to give his vote aloud, on the call of his name, then there would be at least a *possibility* of securing responsibility—to public opinion—on the part of the individual citizen, for his individual public action. There is the point where responsibility—with freedom—should begin in the State.

This direct participation in the common discussions and common action of the regular public meetings of his own fellow-citizens, on his own local affairs, and in the selection of delegates and other public officials, would be the special field of political activity for the ordinary citizen. Political thinkers are generally agreed that this opportunity to take a direct personal part in common public conference as to common public affairs, after reasonable methods, is the fundamental benefit to be obtained from the old-fashioned town meeting. This opportunity, however, would have comparatively little value if citizens even then were to continue, with substantial uniformity, blindly to act under the orders of party leaders and vote for party candidates. The fact is, that between the organization and action of what now exists under the false name of "party," and the organization and free action of a people, as a people, there is an "irrepressible conflict."

The one involves and requires the subordination, almost uniform, of the individual judgment to the commands of the office brokers. The other involves and requires complete freedom of individual thought and action in the process of forming the judgment and will of the people.

The chief reasons for expecting any substantial results from the principles here submitted are to be found, not in the operation of either one of the principles singly, but in the results of all of them combined. If they were all combined, there would be a *possibility* that the citizen could actually enjoy, in practice, something like political freedom. There would be a *possibility* that the election of the highest public officials would involve the free utterance of individual views, and the free exercise of individual judgment, on the merits of individual candidates.

If, too, these considerations be sound, then the adoption of these principles would at least have a *tendency* to secure freedom of political thought and action on the part of the people.

The chief point is, that, at the time of election, the citizens assembled in the public meeting would find it practicable to make new combinations; they could do something more than make a selection from candidates submitted to them beforehand. If the people can be trusted at all, if we can depend on the people at all, under any system, or under any circumstances, to make a wise selection of men for their highest offices, then when a public meeting convened, if any strong combination of men submitted a candidate to that meeting, the meeting could and would adopt that candidate if the requisite number of members were of that mind. If, however, they were not of that mind, then they would have at least the possibility of putting new men in nomination at once, on the spot, at the time, without the formality of "tickets," printed or unprinted.

That is a thing now impossible.

Then, too, if the vote were taken on a call of names, if, too, the discussion were public, if the action of the citizens were public, should we not have, as nearly as that condition of things can be secured by any machinery whatever, that combination of freedom and responsibility as to the action of the individual citizen which would at least have a *tendency* to secure freedom and wisdom of action on the part of the whole people?

If, then, the adoption of these changes would have a tendency, to some extent, to secure freedom of action, to the citizen and to the people, what would be the tendencies as to insuring vigorous and efficient administration from the people's servants?

We have here to consider only *tendencies*. How far these tendencies would operate, I do not here undertake to say. It is enough for the present to consider whether we should make *some* decided *gain;* if so, that is a sufficient reason for making the changes. It is not possible for any system of organization to create or regenerate a people; it can only have *tendencies*, in one or another direction.

The question then is, what would be the tendencies?

If the positions already taken be sound, then the results of the adoption of these changes would *tend* to secure the selection, for the general supervision and control of the public affairs of each people, of each town, city, state, and of the nation, of a body of fairly able men, of varied interests, and of varied opinions. If the people can be trusted to choose men for any of the highest places in the State, if we can really depend on the honesty and good sense of the people, as I confidently believe we can, and as every believer in democratic institutions must hold, then these bodies of men would be bodies that could be safely trusted with that general supervision and control. Being free from the tenure by election, these members would be as free and independent as any body of men in the State. They would have as strong inducements to serve the people faithfully as could be secured with any body of men in the State. Especially they would have *time*—to learn the people's needs, and the measures best suited to meet those needs, and to learn the most efficient ways of doing the large and important work that would come upon them. They would have time—to get experience. They would be continually recruited from the ranks of the people, not from the ranks of hungry adventurers. Steadily, and continuously, new men would take the places made vacant by death and resignation.

Then, too, we should have the best security that is upon the whole practicable, for the selection of a safe and able man for the administrative head. He would be under close and constant responsibility to the popular assembly, a body of men that would, if any body of men could, be able to judge his work well. The popular assembly could remove him, if that were required by the public needs, and keep him in office, so long as the people's interests were best served by keeping him. He would, while being free, yet be under close and constant supervision, and under close and thorough control.

## THE CHANGES NEEDED.

Throughout the executive administration we should have the responsibility, of single individuals, for single classes of work. Each superior would be responsible for the work of his subordinates. If he did not select fit subordinates, or secure from them good practical results, then his superior would be compelled, in self-defence, to remove him.

Throughout the entire public service, from the top to the bottom, the mere personal interest of each official, superior or subordinate, would tend to secure from him the thorough performance of his official work.

But especially the control by the men at the head would be as good as it is practicable to make it.

There would be *at least a tendency* to secure freedom, with responsibility to the people, on the part of our highest public servants.

In the case of these highest public servants— the members of the popular assembly and the administrative head—the responsibility to the popular assembly would be direct and immediate. On the part of subordinate administrative officials, the responsibility to the people would be indirect, through the medium of their superiors. I say this responsibility of subordinates would be indirect. But it would be as direct as is possible, under any system of administration that is practicable. This attempt to enforce direct responsibility to the citizens, or to the people, on the part of any administrative officials other than the one man at the head, must be abandoned as impracticable. Responsibility, that is indirect in form, is all that is practicable, and is the most direct in substance.

Freedom, for our highest officials, is as important as responsibility to the people. Even the people, when it can think and act as a people, must be content to leave to its chief administrative officials a large degree of freedom. Those officials must be free—always within limits; always under supervision and control—to use their own best judgment. Especially they must be free in their selection of their own subordinates. We must give up the idea of tying men's hands, in order to prevent their using official power ill. For by so doing we prevent them from using their power well. Horses cannot run fast when they are hobbled. The head of any administrative force must be responsible; he must be under close and constant supervision, under close and constant control; he must be at any and all times subject to removal at the will of the people, on

## THE CHANGES NEEDED. 153

the judgment of the people. But, being under such supervision and such control, men must be trusted, within the limits of their power, to act on their own judgment. That is a fundamental fact, established by the uniform testimony of all men of large experience in large affairs. " Checks and balances" will not serve our needs. There must be freedom for the public servant, as well as for the individual citizen. When we have those conditions, the selection of a mayor, or a governor, or a president will be a matter of real importance; it will be an affair calling for the exercise of wise judgment, calling for something more than the blind, unquestioning adoption of the action of party managers. When we come, as we shall, to trust men with power, then we shall choose them with care. Then, too, our highest officials, trusted by a people with power, allowed, within lawful and reasonable limits, freedom of action, will not be compelled to obey the money-bags, and will have some reasonable opportunity of earning an honorable reputation by honorable work. They will have the opportunity, with the natural inducements, to serve the people to the best of their ability.

Should we not also get as strong security as is practicable against the purchase of offices and votes?

I do not say that any constitution or laws can altogether prevent such purchases. But with the changes here suggested, if a two-thirds vote of each popular assembly, at each stage of the popular action, were required (as I think it should be) for the selection of any delegate or official, it would be necessary, in order to purchase an office, either to purchase the votes of two thirds of the citizens themselves, at the outset, or the votes of two thirds of the delegates who should be chosen by the people. The purchase of the votes of two thirds of the citizens themselves does not seem to me very probable. The purchase of the votes of two thirds of their delegates would be still more improbable, if we can depend on the people to select men of integrity. And, if we cannot depend on the people to that extent, then we may as well throw up our hands and abandon the contest.

But of that there is no danger. We can depend on the people.

There is one point further.

Can there be, upon the whole, any security against bribery of individual voters so strong as daylight, the requiring each citizen to, utter his voice, openly and above board, in the presence of his fellows? Secrecy has no place in the processes of free democratic government. It is said that employers will endeavor to coerce their employees, that rich men will attempt to coerce poor men. Such attempts, if made, will be made only by those employers and those rich men who prefer to use the methods of corruption. If those men can only be known, their game will soon be ended. Now the best security for finding them out will be the publicity of the public meeting.

With public offices held, and public affairs administered, on such a basis, we should have at least some *possibility* of a vigorous and wise administration of our public affairs.

In short, the adoption of these principles would, I submit, give at least *some possibility*, and would have *some tendency*, to secure freedom of political thought and action for both citizens and people, and, at the same time, to secure good administration.

Would not that be something of an advance?

Nevertheless, even if the considerations thus far submitted should carry some degree of conviction to the mind of the reader, many men will shrink from remedies so radical, and will incline to seek refuge in reforms more partial.

Let us, therefore, next consider whether any

of the "reforms" now prominently proposed afford any reasonable promise of any lasting or substantial relief from the evils that now afflict the body politic.

The evils, it will be conceded, are serious and radical. The remedies, therefore, we may safely assume, must be strong and searching. They must deal with the disease at its roots. They must not trifle with surface symptoms. We must have what Cromwell's men called "root-and-branch" work.

And first let us examine what is termed "Civil Service Reform."

In its entire length and breadth, in its fullest scope, taking it on the statement of its most enthusiastic friends, it consists in putting some restrictions, and supposed securities, around the power of appointment of subordinate administrative officers.

How adequate is such a proposal to existing needs?

Here is a people engaged in an attempt to establish a democratic government. And the situation that we find is, that a powerful privileged class, of political adventurers, controls the action of the citizen and the people, the selection and official action of presidents, congressmen, governors, members of the state legislatures, and mayors, buying and selling our highest offices, like merchandise, for money.

In such a position we are recommended to require examinations and tests, merely preliminary, for the lowest grades of administrative officials.

Men say that this is a beginning—in the right direction.

But we must begin at the right point. When we wish to purify a stream that has become foul, we begin not at the mouth, but at its source. And when we wish to operate on large masses of men, we must deal with the men at their head.

But let us examine this "Reform" further.

The substantial test as to fitness, for the actual work of any office, must be made in the office itself, and at the work of the office itself. Preliminary tests, as to mere knowledge of facts of any kind, are well enough in their way. They will be made by any sensible superior, who is held to a close responsibility for results, if he is free to conduct his office after his own methods. But the only test or examination that can have substantial value must be made in the work of the office and by the superior.

Moreover, the tests that are merely preliminary can be made best by the superior, and should be made by him. They can be made well by no one but a person having a close and intimate knowledge of the precise work to be done.

But the plan of "Civil Service Reform" is to have these preliminary examinations made by persons outside the administrative offices, by persons, therefore, who probably have themselves no special knowledge of the special work of the special officials who are to be examined. The examiners will, in all probability, therefore, be generally unable to do well the work of mere preliminary examination.

But that is not all. Until a substantial change is made in the selection and the tenure of our highest officials, there is no reasonable possibility that this "Reform," even within its limited scope, can be carried out. The officials *at the head*, whose personal interest under present methods constantly presses them to keep the power they have, will use their strongest efforts to prevent the "Reform" from becoming a success. And without the earnest co-operation of those highest officials, it cannot be made a success. Give them their freedom, and they will devise and carry out wise tests for the fitness of their subordinates. But we must make it serve their personal interests so to do. In short, whichever way we turn, we run against this fundamental fact, that, in order to get any substantial improvement in present methods, we must operate, not on the men at the bottom, but on the men at the head; and, until we do so, no substantial or lasting change for the better is to be expected.

The proposed scheme is flatly in conflict with well-established principles of administration. If a banker is to have his office well administered, he must have the free selection and the full control of his subordinates. The same proposition is true as to an engineer, a postmaster, the head of the entire postal service, the head of a customhouse, or the head of any single office or single department. The proposition rests on the facts of human nature. Subordinates must feel that, within lawful limits, they owe their selection for, and their retention of, their places to their official superior. They must feel, at all times, that they are under his immediate supervision and his direct control. He must, no doubt, be held to strict responsibility. But that must be our security for his right use of his official power. If we tie his hands, we make it impossible for him to use his power for good as well as for evil.

Security lies in responsibility, of an official who is free, not in fetters.

It is said, too, that by taking these minor offices out of "politics," we diminish the power of the professional politicians, and make it, at least to some extent, less possible for them to pay for election work.

Now it is, no doubt, the fact that the minor offices are used, to some extent, to pay for election work. But they are used to pay only the subordinates. They will continue to be so used until we deal effectually with the superiors.

But what is it proposed to do, as to the use of all the *superior offices ;* and as to those millions of dollars that are paid by men who pay their money for "political purposes" before election, and who get their own individual interests so well served, by officials who ought to serve only the people, after election? I concede that the friends of "Civil Service Reform" have done a very valuable public service, in arousing the public mind to the necessity of destroying the "spoils system" as to minor offices. But, if it is important to destroy that system as to minor offices, it is all the more important to destroy it as to the offices at the head. And it is with those offices at the head that we must make our beginning. The "spoils system" cannot be rooted out as to the minor offices, until it is rooted out as to the higher ones.

But if the "Reform" could be carried out to the letter, in its full length and breadth, it would be a mere drop in the bucket. The results would be too inconsiderable to deserve serious attention. It is wholly inadequate to meet the fundamental existing evils.

We come next to a consideration of what is generally termed the "Australian Ballot System."

The chief feature of this system is, that it is an effort to secure still greater isolation and secrecy in the action of the individual citizen. It is an attempt to protect the individual citizen from influence, of any kind, good or bad, at the moment of his depositing a secret ballot in the ballot-box. To that end it proposes to put the citizen himself in a box. It proposes also to have "tickets" or "ballots" printed at the expense of the State. The theory is, that this will do something, or much, to prevent the use of corrupt influences with the citizen, especially the corrupt use of money.

But here again, what a grotesque disproportion between the disease and the remedy! The amount, and the continuous regularity, of this election work, which constitute the producing cause of these standing armies, remain untouched. The citizen will still be compelled, if he wishes his vote to count, to vote for the candidates of one of the large armies. He will still continue to be loyal to his own army, to dislike deserters, and to surrender his freedom of individual judgment and action at the dictation of his party leaders. He will still continue to be the political puppet.

The bribery question is, I submit, equally unimportant; I mean, when it is viewed in its true proportions. The use of money in the purchase of individual voters, its use in retail, is, I believe, considerably exaggerated. However that may be, our chief concern is not with its use at retail, but its use at wholesale, its use in controlling *nominations*, not of one party, but of all parties; its use in the virtual purchase of votes by the thousands, hundreds of thousands, and the million. So long as we leave the control of all our highest officials in the hands of the men who supply the party treasuries, who virtually buy votes by the million, in advance, it is not an economy of time to give much thought to the purchase of single voters on the day of election. If we are to depend on putting the citizen in a box, we must box him long before election day.

## THE CHANGES NEEDED.

The advocates of this especial scheme attach much importance to the fact that the State is to pay the cost of printing ballots.

But the cost of printing ballots is comparatively trifling; even in the largest cities it is only a few thousands of dollars. But how is it as to these hundreds of thousands of dollars that are used *before* election day and *after* election day for "political purposes"—in other words, for the virtual purchase of officials and official action.

What we need to consider is, not the purchase of a few thousand votes of individual voters, so much as the sale of the offices at the head, the purchase of legislatures, and the millions stolen from the public treasuries, at every hand, *after election*.

But, if there be any soundness in the positions before taken, this separation of the individual citizen, at the very time when he is to take political action, this secrecy of the action of the citizen, this protecting him from influence, all rest on unsound grounds and on erroneous theories of democratic government.

Publicity is of its very essence. Influence of one citizen by another, by fair, reasonable, open, public argument, is of its very essence. Responsibility of the individual citizen, for his individual action, is of its very essence. All these require publicity. Publicity, too, is the strongest security that is practicable against bribery.

I submit, then, that the so-called "Australian system" is fundamentally unsound in principle, is an attempt to deal only with surface symptoms, and should be put in the category of petty political panaceas.

Another proposed measure, which has frequently received very reputable support, is that the heads of administrative departments should have seats in the popular assembly (or in one branch of the popular assembly, where there are two), and should there be required from time to time to answer questions as to their department administration.

This is especially urged as a means of enforcing administrative responsibility.

It is commonly said that this feature has been tried in Great Britain, and "works well."

If there is one nation among civilized peoples especially distinguished for administrative inefficiency, except in some departments which are practically free from the operation of this feature, it is Great Britain.

The reasons are not hard to find. In a popular assembly charged with the general supervision and control of the entire affairs of a large people, it is quite impracticable to give full and sufficient statements of the details of department work in mere oral debate, or oral conference. Such statements can be given only in full and carefully prepared reports, in print, with full details of facts and figures. Not only is it impracticable for such reports to be made in any other form than in print, but in no other form can they be properly examined and studied.

Moreover, the head of a large executive department, who has to superintend and control the operations of a large number of subordinates, must give his time and work to his department. As an ingenious device for wasting time and human strength, nothing can well be conceived more efficient than this favorite of literary politicians, the asking and answering of questions on the floor of the popular assembly.

It is simply impossible, for any head of a large department, who does his work well, to give any considerable amount of time to defending his "policy" in a deliberative assembly. Very probably, if he be a man of action, he will not be a man of words. If he is to have a "policy" worth defending, his time and toil, his days and nights, must be given to making that "policy," not in making speeches about it. Human life is not long enough, human strength is not strong enough, to enable one man, as a rule, to manage a great state department and also take part in the conferences of a working deliberative assembly. If his keeping his place is to depend on the results of parliamentary contests, over parliamentary questions, then, I concede, his presence will be necessary in the parliamentary assembly. Then, too, it will matter little how well he does the work of administration. But if his administrative work is to be done, and done well, that work must have his time and thought. His responsibility must be for his administrative work, to his administrative superiors, not for forcible argument in a deliberative assembly.

Then, too, even now, it may be said that citizens should give greater attention to "politics," should attend the "party" primary meetings, and seek reform, within the existing political "parties," by existing methods.

But this has been often tried in the past, and has always failed. It will certainly and always fail in the future, unless we can find some way to enable amateurs to beat professionals, or some way by which ordinary men, who have to earn their living, can give all their time to "politics," and yet give all their time to the regular occupation by which they gain their bread. The best men in the community are the men who work, who are, for one or another reason, compelled to work, who work hard at some regular calling. Now if some one will devise a way by which these men *who do the work* of society can at the same time give large amounts of time to this work of managing caucuses and elections—in short, if we can make each one of these citizens "two gentlemen at once"—then there may be some possibility of getting good government work out of our present election machine.

But it may be suggested that we can have longer official terms.

This suggestion will be found, on careful consideration, to overlook the essential reason, and the necessary result, of any and every system of fixed terms of office, of whatever length.

The purpose of the term system in any form, with terms of any length, is to keep the highest officials under the control of the citizens.

Now this purpose of using the term system at all requires that the term be short. The purpose is to have the official under the control of the citizen all the time, or as nearly so as is practicable. If, then, the term be long, assuming that such control were really secured by having a term of any length, the official will be virtually freed from this control of the citizen for the greater part of the term. For the more distant the election, the more independent is the official, and the more he will count on *time* to do away with the unpopularity that might come to him from some of his official acts.

But a term that is long at its beginning becomes short near its end. And then the evils continually increase. Then comes the inevitable slavery to the election machine, and to the rich and powerful interests that control it. So that a longer term loses the assumed advantages, and keeps the actual disadvantages, of a term that is short.

Moreover, even if it should be supposed that a single official, standing by himself, would be somewhat more independent if his term were longer, yet no substantial improvement would be gained if all the highest officials still continued to hold their offices under terms of some length. For they would all still be dependent on carrying elections; vacancies in all these offices would still be certain, and would come at fixed periods; the mass of election work would still be large, continuous, and regular; it would still be in the hands of professionals; and those professionals would still, in one way or another, select and control the officials. We should make no substantial gain in emancipating the citizen, the people, or the public servant.

Turn it as we may, the fact remains, and cannot in any way be avoided, that the individual citizens, educated and uneducated alike, in general, are, and always must be, incompetent to form an intelligent judgment on the official action of public officials, except in the local affairs that come under the cognizance of the town, and other local, primary meetings; that, in the larger peoples of larger numbers, the members of the supreme popular assembly will be the only men in the State who can possibly have the knowledge necessary to form an intelligent judgment as to the official conduct of any member of the assembly or the chief executive; and that the attempt to secure responsibility, on the part of those members, or of the chief executive, to the body of citizens, through tenure by election, for fixed terms of years, either short or long, necessarily and certainly fails to accomplish that result, but on the contrary does necessarily and certainly turn government into an election machine.

This term system, in any and all its forms, is

the result of attempts to work out a rough rudimentary idea of democratic government, in the form of government by the individual citizens. Mr. Lincoln struck a grand phrase when he spoke of " government of the people, by the people, for the people." But to put that idea into practice, if we are to give the words all the meaning of which they are susceptible, and which they ought to carry, is a thing yet to be accomplished. To put in practical form the idea that this great combination of states, formerly, as between themselves, independent, is a single living organism, that it must have unity of existence, unity of organization, and, above all, unity of brain and will—to work out that idea in practical form, to make it a living, accomplished fact, that is a work of magnitude, to be undertaken and accomplished by this American people, after its simple, old-fashioned methods, by the regular machinery provided by law, a machinery often before used, and always with marked success, the Constitutional Convention.

But some persons, even if they are convinced that the points here presented are sound " theoretically," yet will be strongly inclined to the opinion that the points cannot be put into practice.

Why not ?

The undertaking will not be as hard as was the formation of a single national government, by the inhabitants of thirteen different colonies, some of them of different blood, habits of thought, and religion, with the strongest fears of any government except their own colonial legislatures, who had just thrown off the yoke of a foreign king, and whose citizens, in general, had the most petty, provincial ideas. Consider, too, that that undertaking was accomplished without the railroad or the telegraph, and virtually without the press and the post-office; in other words, almost wholly without the modern highways of thought. We are apt to forget the difficulties under which the men labored who framed our national Constitution and procured its adoption, and the great facilities we now have for forming a great national idea and a great national sentiment, and putting that idea and sentiment into practical forms. If the principles here set forth are sound, a point which can be determined only after full and free public discussion, then it will be much easier to amend the national Constitution than it was to make it. It will be much easier for this now consolidated people to make some changes in its political organization than it was to get an organization, or to get and keep a mere political existence. Let us remember how we came into being, when we came into being, and what we have done in these years during which we have only reached our political majority, while we have been cutting our political teeth, and having our political mumps and measles. Bearing these points in mind, who will venture to say that the work of amending our political system in all necessary points is beyond the capacity of this people?

The main ground, however, on which would rest the impression that the changes which are necessary cannot be adopted in practice would probably be the idea that those changes would be opposed by the professional politicians.

Even, if that were so, it would constitute no good reason for not making the effort, provided the changes are necessary. If the principles here urged are sound, they are sure, in time, to be adopted. And be it remembered that political forces are larger, and political growth is more rapid, with us, at this time, than with any other people, or at any former time. Political events with us move with great speed. If it were the fact, therefore, that these changes would be opposed by the professional politicians, that would be no good reason why we should not at least make an effort to improve our methods of government.

But is it so certain that these ideas would be opposed by the professionals?

As a single individual, my own present view is, that we should do wisely if we were to put our modified system of government into operation by adopting it with the men who are at the time already in office; that is, we should abolish the term system at once for all officials, make all the administrative officials directly responsible to their immediate superiors, make the chief executive directly responsible to the legislature— removable by a concurrent two-thirds vote of both houses—and then provide that the new method of election by the process of the public meeting be adopted only in the selection of public officers to be chosen as the successors of men already in office.

I should urge this for two reasons:

The first is, that such a step would be best for the highest public interests. It would introduce proper administrative methods and efficient men, in the shortest time practicable. Among the men now in office there is a large number of able men, men who are very desirous of doing good work, and who would do it if we allowed them. Many of them have a fair amount of experience. These men now in office are in a measure representative men, as much so as any similar number of men whom we have any reasonable chance of getting under the present system. The men in office at the time, therefore, seem to me, upon the whole, the best body of men that it is at present practicable for us to obtain, in whose hands to trust our government work; in other words, they would constitute the best body of men that we could reasonably expect to get, with whom to make our experiment of common-sense business methods.

The second reason is, that, on this plan, we could probably command the support of the professional politicians to such a modification of our political system. I mean, if the ideas here presented are sound. Even the professional politicians have in their composition a large proportion of human nature; and they are very willing and eager to serve popular interests, and especially to fall in with popular ideas—so long as it is not necessary at the same time to sacrifice their own personal interests.

Now these proposed changes would, first and foremost, directly and especially serve the personal interests of the most powerful professional politicians of both the present so-called political "parties." The most powerful men of both parties at this time are those who are now in office. They number about as many of one party as of the other. Together they form only one "party," of two parts. They have been long accustomed to working and trading together, in great harmony. The only point of difference between them consists in their "platforms." But each makes the same use of its "platform." They parade it before election, and use it for a war-dance after election.

This plan, therefore, of doing away with the term system, for all men at the time in office, happens not only to be for the highest public interests of the people, but it would also, directly and immediately, most effectively serve the personal interests of all these professionals.

It would command their support. That is surely a strong consideration in its favor.

And has any scheme yet been presented to the public mind for the improvement of administrative methods that combined all these features? that *even appeared* to have a tendency to accomplish the emancipation of the citizen, of the people, and of the public servant?—in short, to serve the highest public interests of both citizen and people, and at the same time serve the personal interests of the professional politicians of both the present prominent political parties?

Let me put another question.

Is there not at least an approach to a possibility that our present public servants, even assuming that we never had better men, would give us better work under a better system than they can give us under our present one?

## SOME GENERAL CONSIDERATIONS.

But it may be said, all this is mere "theorizing."

The discussion of our present national Constitution, when it was under consideration in the Constitutional Convention, was mere "theorizing."

It must be conceded that the members of that Convention "theorized" to some purpose.

Let us look at our present political position.

Our present position is, that something must be *done*.

Then the question is, what is the right thing to do? Whoever objects to what is here proposed can fairly be called on to propose something better. It is not greatly to our purpose to give a vivacious and interesting account of mere phenomena; to put in readable form a statement of the present and past working of our political institutions.

In its way that is very well.

But what are we to *do*—in the future? Events will not stand still, even if we men may wish to do so.

We cannot, and shall not, let our political fortunes drift at the mercy of the political winds and waves. We have to study the charts, find out the rocks and shoals, learn, as far as we can, all the points of danger, and then, as far as human foresight avails to that end, we must lay out the course of our future political voyage *beforehand*, according to our best knowledge and judgment. Many men are inclined, when any scheme of political organization, or reorganization, is advanced for public consideration, to sneer at it as "theoretical," and to say that these things cannot be "planned beforehand;" that constitutions are *not drafted on paper*, but they *must grow*.

This kind of criticism comes usually from men who have not taken the time, or given the hard work, necessary for a full comprehension of the real points of the political problem. No doubt, in one sense, the careful consideration of any fundamental modification of our political system is "theorizing."

But the formation, or amendment, of every state constitution, of every city and town charter, is a piece of political "theorizing" of precisely this same kind. We Americans are, of all things, a nation of "political theorizers." We are not believers in political patch-work. We are, by nature and education, "constitution-makers." We are the political descendants of the men who came over in the *Mayflower*. They were the men who first in the history of the world formed, by their common deliberations, a paper constitution, a political compact, of limited scope, of vague form, but yet a written constitution, drawn up *beforehand, on paper*, under which a great people began its political existence. I confess to a strong admiration for the political work and the political methods of that little body of men, who furnished the first example in the work of making "paper constitutions," an example which has been since followed with such uniformity by the American people, in the drafting, and adoption, and amendment of charters and constitutions for its towns, cities, states, and the nation.

The practice is not now to be abandoned.

Especially are we given to political experiment. The consideration of any new scheme of government, or of any proposal for the modification of any old scheme of government, must necessarily be "theoretical;" that is, it must be based on ideas—on ideas of what political means are necessary to produce certain political ends. What those means are, always is and always must be, inevitably, to some extent, matter of speculation, of conjecture, of "theory." But with this American people the practical political question of the day is, shall we continue to use a "theory" which we have thoroughly tried, which we know has already failed in the past, and will certainly fail in the future, or shall we make the attempt to devise some new political process, or some new combination of old processes? If we conclude, as we certainly shall, to attempt something new, in this new land of new things, of new political forces and new political processes, what shall it be? And how are we to decide? There is only one way possible, and that is to study the past, to study human nature—the material which we must use—and to work out a "theory," an idea—or a set of ideas. We must discuss them in public, turn them over, put them under our mental microscopes, and then work out a scheme, a system. For this body politic is a very delicate organism, one that requires careful handling; if we change its laws of life at one point, we may need to change them at other points.

But change, of some kind, we undoubtedly must make, fundamental and constitutional.

We must give up our system of distrust of public servants. We must finally realize that governments, as well as other organizations of human beings, must be managed on the basis of confidence in men. We all know that single individuals, here and there, under the stress of temptation, prove faithless to the trusts they un-undertake. As a rule, however, men who are selected with care are faithful, and do their work as well as they know how. Their errors are largely errors of ignorance. All the vast operations of commerce, all private affairs, are, and must be, transacted on the basis of confidence in human nature. On no other basis can the world move. We are compelled to act on this basis now, in our administration of public affairs under our present system.

But we must act on this basis throughout. We must realize that all our public affairs must be administered by men. Those men must be surrounded by the same safeguards with which prudent men surround their servants in private life. We must select them with the greatest care; we must give them the same opportunities to gain skill and experience; we must keep them under careful supervision and control; and we must provide the proper means for securing their full responsibility to the people. But, having done all this, we must give them our confidence, knowing that in individual instances it will be abused, but that in the large majority of cases our public servants will serve us faithfully, if they are only free.

The more we think of it, the more strong will be our disbelief in astronomical politics; or in any political system under which public officials are put in and out of office at fixed periods of time—after any fixed number of revolutions of this or any other planet around this or any other sun. If men were apples or pumpkins, if they ripened and decayed with the seasons of this star which we term the earth, then it might be conceded that we could properly fix their terms of service by the same periods of time that fixed their ripening and decay. But men are not so constituted. And it would seem natural and reasonable that the times of their appointment to, and removal from, public offices, should have some relation to the times of their fitness and unfitness for the public service. In private affairs we select men for certain kinds of work on account of their fitness, actual or supposed, for those kinds of work; we keep them in our employ so long as they do their work well; and we discharge them when, for any reason, they do

## SOME GENERAL CONSIDERATIONS. 183

their work ill. We know, too, that men, if they are of the right kind, if we have been wise in our selection, until very late in life, improve with time; they get greater skill, greater prudence, greater wisdom; each year makes them more valuable servants, at least for the higher positions of supervision and control. For the less responsible work of execution we need the stronger muscles and greater physical vigor of youth. But in the high positions of supervision and control we need men who have gained wisdom, from long experience in the administration of public affairs.

Now the very essence of the astronomical system is, that we cannot have men of wisdom and experience in the highest public places. For, if any public official does his duty to the people, faithfully and fearlessly, he is certain of being in time removed from the public service. It is not that the people do not wish him longer to serve them, or that he does not wish longer to serve the people, or even that the professional politicians do not wish to give us as good public service as the system allows. But no one is free; the people is not free; the official is not free; the politicians are not free. All are bound by this overpowering necessity of carrying on this monstrous astronomical election machine. Free democratic government is made impossible.

We must change the system; so that the citizens can have freedom of action; so that the people can have freedom of action; so that the officials can have freedom of action, with thorough and constant responsibility to the people; and finally, so that the people may be ruled by the people's brain.

The actual working of our present system is, that the servants appoint themselves, instead of being appointed by the people; the servants rule the people, instead of the people ruling the servants. If we judge political systems by their practical results, our system is not democratic. It may be such in form; it is not so in its working results.

But working results are what is required by this practical American people. And, as a working result, what we have accomplished thus far is, with some democratic features, a combination of ochlocracy and plutocracy—a rule of mob and money—greatly restrained, no doubt, by public opinion, or, speaking more correctly, by public sentiment. For on any specific public question of actual, practical public affairs, the people is not now so organized that it can form and utter anything that can properly be called an "opinion"—"of the people." The will of the people is not supreme. For we have no adequate political machinery, under our present imperfect organization, for its formation or its expression. The only organ it now has is, substantially, the press; and, great as is the power of the press, admirable as has been its service, it is not capable of serving as the people's brain and will in the actual daily administration of public affairs. The people's present political life is a continued contest for place, between large combinations of individuals, to serve personal ends, instead of being one continuous, harmonious, co-operative expenditure of the combined energy of one people, organized to act as one body, under one mind and will, to serve public ends, so far as that result is practicable by merely human means, by merely human machinery.

The doing of our public work demands a large brain and a strong hand; a larger brain and a stronger hand than the brain and hand of any single individual or single faction. It demands, too, something more than the sporadic thought of an imperfectly organized mass of individual citizens, even if they be orderly and law-abiding, and take part each year in what is termed a "popular election." The work demands, too, something better than the alternating will of factions, constantly engaged in a struggle for public place. In short, the work can be done satisfactorily only by the mind and hand of the people—the whole people—thinking and acting as one people, thinking *at the time it acts*, on the *man or measure on which* it is to act. Something more is needed than an annual battle with ballots between two great contending armies. This American people, made up of individuals and smaller peoples, must be organized—organized rightly. It must cease to be a comparatively disorganized collection of mere individuals. Each people must have its own head and its own hand. It must administer its own affairs. But it must be organized as one people. Our public work is now too vast, our public interests are now too large, to be handled on the rotatory principle—to have their control put up year after year as the prize of these great election contests, and put alternately into the hands of one and another faction of professional politicians, whose time and efforts are continually given to the management of these vast election campaigns. Public work calls for the highest wisdom and administrative talent that the people can command. It cannot be done, if it is to be done well, by merely ordinary men, of merely ordinary knowledge, of ordinary experience, taken from time to time from the ranks of the citizens, to serve for only one, two, ten, or even twenty years, and then to be dropped back again into the mass of citizens, it may be in the midst of a great negotiation, or even of a great war. Astronomical politics served fairly well as a first experiment in the science of popular government. It is, no doubt, a great advance on the tyranny of irresponsible hereditary kings and hereditary classes. It may even now answer, passably, for the affairs of a people that has small numbers and little wealth. One can drive with comparative ease and safety on a corduroy road, with light weights and at low speed. But when we use the large masses, large forces, and large velocities of a great and complex modern society, then we must have the strongest and smoothest machinery and the best methods that modern political science can devise. We must have a solid political road-bed, carefully graded, with political steel rails, and all the best appliances that can be provided by the wisdom of the whole people. When we talk of "government by the people," in these days, we mean something more than that this great mass of individual citizens shall be the pawns on the political chessboard, in the great game of "politics" as now played. We mean that these citizens shall do something more than serve as the automatic digits in a great election machine, to put printed lists in a box, even if the machine be operated without a jar, in strict accordance with the forms of law. To call this thing "government by the people" is not an accurate use of words.

I have it fully in mind that government is to be something more than a mere organization of the people, for the mere transaction of the people's business on ordinary business principles. It must also secure to the individual citizen, and to the whole people, the fullest measure of healthy political activity and political freedom; it must, so far as such things can be as yet secured by human institutions, secure to every individual citizen, to each smaller people, and to the whole nation, a free, vigorous, healthy political life.

But the accomplishment of those ends is entirely consistent with vigorous and efficient administration. More than that, the same changes that are needed to accomplish the one result are indispensable in order to accomplish the other. In such an organization as is necessary for such a people as ours, if our public affairs are to be administered with wisdom and efficiency, it is needless to say that the different classes of the public work must be in the hands of men of training, especially of that kind of training that can be gained only by long experience. Potatoes and beets come to their full, mature growth in one or two years. For fruits and vegetables the year system may be well. But human beings, as yet developed, need a lifetime—the time of human, not potato, life—to get their growth. Let us rid ourselves, finally and forever, of this antiquated maiden fancy, that men can serve the people well without training and experience, and can reach the full measure of their usefulness in two, four, or ten years.

Now, has not the experience of the human race, especially has not this experience of our own during the last one hundred years, definitely settled some political laws, that must be observed in the organization of any democratic government, that is to be a practical working success?

If so, what are those laws?

Have they been here stated with accuracy?

THE END.

# POLITICS FOR YOUNG AMERICANS.

Politics for Young Americans. By CHARLES NORDHOFF. 16mo, Half Leather, 75 cents; Paper, 40 cents.

It would be difficult to find, indeed, a safer guide for a young man getting ready to "cast his first ballot."—*Nation*, N. Y.

A short and very clear account of the reason of governments, the things which government can and ought to do, and the things which it cannot do and ought not to attempt, and the principles which ought to prevail in its treatment, by legislation or administration, of the things which properly come within its province. It is thus a treatise of political ethics and of political economy, and an excellent one.—*N. Y. World*.

It is a book that should be in the hand of every American boy and girl. This book of Mr. Nordhoff's might be learned by heart. . . . It is a complete system of political science, economical and other, as applied to our American system.—*N. Y. Herald*.

A book based upon an excellent idea, which is admirably carried out in its contents. The book, though intended for the young, will by no means find its usefulness confined to that sphere. The elementary knowledge of this volume, therefore, will prove of general value. We commend it to universal reading and study.—*Saturday Evening Gazette*, Boston.

Here is a book which we wish could be put into the hands of every boy in the United States, and, for that matter, into the hands of a majority of the men, too; for of the first principles of political science which it lays down the majority of our voters have but a dim idea, if any at all. . . . Mr. Nordhoff's style is fresh, vigorous, and compact, and he has a knack of stating political and economic truths in such an epigrammatic way that they are at once recognized and are easily retained.—*San Francisco Post*.

Written in the lucid, compact, and weighty style which belongs to the pen of the author. Mr. Nordhoff has but few superiors in the use of a solid and forcible English. The great essentials of the American system of political, economical, and social life are embraced in this work, and so treated as to make not only a readable, but also an exceedingly instructive book, well adapted to be useful to all classes.—*Independent*, N. Y.

None can deny the practised ability, the pleasing perspicuity, and the general excellence of Mr. Nordhoff's work.—*Christian Advocate*, N. Y.

---

PUBLISHED BY HARPER & BROTHERS, NEW YORK.

☞ HARPER & BROTHERS *will send the above work by mail, postage prepaid, to any part of the United States or Canada, on receipt of the price.*

# BY ALBERT STICKNEY.

Democratic Government. A Study of Politics. By ALBERT STICKNEY. Post 8vo, Cloth, $1 00.

It has the merit of independent, earnest, and original conviction. It is throughout thoroughly American, and shows the democratic training that has made New England life so forceful in all parts of this country.... The book will arouse interest because of its freshness and evident and sensible patriotism.—*Philadelphia Times.*

Mr. Stickney is thoroughly convinced that our present Constitution does not meet the requirements of this nation, and his reasons for so thinking he has given with great energy and clearness.... Mr. Stickney is an unusually stimulating and suggestive writer.—*Rochester Democrat and Chronicle.*

\ The exposition of the evil of professional politicians, of ring rule politics, and of divided responsibility should be read by every citizen. —*N. Y. Herald.*

It is the aim of this volume to show that there is a remedy, and that this is in simply returning to a truly popular representative government.... The volume will surely be accepted as a valuable contribution to the political thought of the time.—*N. Y. Times.*

A clear, vigorous discussion of practical politics.... It is one of many signs that people are thinking to the point, as well as a help to students to formulate their own vague notions.—*Atlantic Monthly,* Boston.

An intelligently and forcibly considered study in politics, deals temperately, justly, vigorously, and from the stand-point of a consistent and conscientious Democrat with the principles, precepts, and practice of democracy in its intended purity and impartial administration of justice.—*New Orleans Times Democrat.*

A True Republic. By ALBERT STICKNEY. Post 8vo, Cloth, $1 00.

An important political treatise worthy to be read and studied on both sides of the Atlantic.... Will amply repay perusal.—*Literary World,* London.

Mr. Stickney writes well and forcibly, and some of his propositions are undeniably true.... His elegantly made and interesting book will be classed with the Utopia of Sir Thomas More and the Republic of Plato.—*N. Y. Evening Mail.*

Mr. Stickney's book will be found very suggestive. He sketches the different kinds of government people have lived under, and reviews our own. Every thinking American should read it.—*N. Y. Commercial Advertiser.*

---

PUBLISHED BY HARPER & BROTHERS, NEW YORK.

☞ *The above works sent by mail, postage prepaid, to any part of the United States, Canada, or Mexico, on receipt of the price.*

www.ingramcontent.com/pod-product-compliance
Lightning Source LLC
Chambersburg PA
CBHW021734220426
43662CB00008B/847